151

Quick Ideas

to
Manage Your Time

By Robert E. Dittmer, APR

CAREER
PRESS
Franklin Lakes, NJ

151 QUICK IDEAS TO MANAGE YOUR TIME
EDITED BY JODI BRANDON
TYPESET BY GINA TALUCCI
Cover design by The Visual Group
Printed in the U.S.A. by Book-mart Press

To order this title, please call toll-free 1-800-CAREER-1 (NJ and Canada: 201-848-0310) to order using VISA or MasterCard, or for further information on books from Career Press.

The Career Press, Inc., 3 Tice Road, PO Box 687,
Franklin Lakes, NJ 07417
www.careerpress.com

Library of Congress Cataloging-in-Publication Data

Dittmer, Robert E., 1950-
    151 quick ideas to manage your time / by Bob Dittmer
        p. cm.
    ISBN-13: 978-1-56414-899-5
    ISBN-10: 1-56414-899-8
        1. Time management. I. Title. II. One hundred fifty-one quick ideas
to manage your time.

HD69.T54D52 2006
650.1′1--dc22

                                                             2006016820

Dedication

To all the people over the past 30-plus years who have worked with me, shared with me, taught me, suffered with me, to cause me to learn these lessons and be able to share them with others.

And, to Jerry Wilson, CSP. Client, mentor, friend, partner.

You led the way, I merely follow.

Contents

How to Use This Book

Every quick idea in this book has been selected to directly or indirectly help you gain and retain customers, create relationships, and build a successful business.

Don't try to implement all 151 ideas at once, because some won't be a good fit right now. Read through all 151 quick ideas and select only those that can really make a difference at the moment. Don't worry, you'll go back and review the others periodically.

Label your ideas…

◆ Implement now.

◆ Review again in 30 days.

◆ Pass the idea along to _____.

Involve your staff in selecting and implementing these ideas, and don't forget to give credit for their success! Invest in additional copies of this book and distribute them among your staff. Get everyone involved in selecting and recommending various quick ideas.

Revisit this book every 90 days. As your business changes, you will find new quick ideas that might suit you better now that competition is heating up.

Remember, all the ideas in this book have been proven in businesses across the United States and around the world. They have worked for others and will work for you!

Introduction:
This Book Can Save You Time!

Every quick idea in this book has been selected to directly or indirectly help you save time and stress through better organization, better time management, and better people management.

Don't try to implement all 151 ideas, because some won't be exactly right for you. Read through all 151 quick ideas and select only those that can really make a big difference in your life. Label your ideas:

◆ Implement now.

◆ Review again in 30 days (or 60 or 90 days).

◆ Pass the idea along to _____.

Sometimes, involving your staff in selecting and implementing some of these ideas will not only help you, but help them as well. Invest in some additional copies of this book and distribute them among your staff as required reading. Get everyone involved in selecting and recommending quick ideas. If everyone uses his or her time better, your life will also be improved.

Revisit this book every few months. As your situation changes and new work and tasks come your way, you will find quick ideas you bypassed today that will save you time tomorrow.

Remember: All 151 ideas in this book have been proven by people similar to you all across the United States and around the world. They work! *But you must implement and follow through with each one you choose*. Do that, and you will be rewarded with more time and less stress in your life. And isn't that why you bought this book in the first place?

1

Getting Started Is the Toughest Step

Just as people become addicted to drugs, food, cigarettes, and other such pastimes, people get addicted to the go-go lifestyles we all seem to live these days. My neighbor with three teenagers is constantly speaking proudly about her ability to manage multiple schedules and tasks and get it all done. Unfortunately, in the next breath, she also complains about never having enough time, about her day being totally fragmented to the point she can never concentrate on anything fully, and about never being able to spend "quality time" with her family.

It wasn't until recently that she came to understand, unfortunately the hard way, that she needed to better control her time schedule instead of allowing it to control her. You see, the stress finally got to her and she became severely ill—the result, according to the doctor, of being on the go too much. Of course, not only did she suffer the illness (she has recovered nicely, thank you), but so too did her family suffer.

And it did not need to happen!

Assignment

Decide to get started evaluating YOUR lifestyle before you too have to go through an event the way my neighbor did. Take a look at your daily schedule and you'll discover not only how hectic it is, but also places where you can save time and trouble.

She used this "event" to analyze her lifestyle and daily routine and decided she needed to get a better handle on it. She now confesses to being a "reformed" time-a-holic (her words). But it was too dramatic of an event in her life to bring her to this realization. Many of us cannot afford such a dramatic event. So just as an alcoholic does, it's time to assess—or reassess—our priorities.

Epilogue

My neighbor used this illness as a warning and as a new beginning. She evaluated her lifestyle and time management and began anew managing her time better. She reports that her health is better and her time with her family has increased, and yet she still accomplishes everything that is important to her every day.

2

Consider a Time Study

The first thing my neighbor did to change her life was conduct a time study. No, she did not call it that, but that is what she did. Once she was able, she started a logbook of all of her daily activities. She recorded everything she did every day for two weeks. All the details.

Assignment

Consider this simple time study technique. It's not fancy and doesn't require you to have any assets you don't already have. But you will learn a great deal from it.

Everything she did, including when she went to the rest room, and who stopped by when, and the gory details of every meeting and appointment.

She kept times on all of these so she could go back later and find out what took what amount of time and, in many cases, because she kept excellent details, why it took that much time.

After two weeks, she had enough data. She spent a few hours making notes on what she learned as she reviewed her logbook. This was her analysis. Not scientific, no, but very useful. She learned a lot about how she spent her time.

Epilogue

There are companies who require their employees to keep time study records so the company as a whole can examine time usage and make adjustments to its systems and procedures. If it works for them, this simple mechanism can work for you.

3

Assess Your Problem Areas

Now that you've conducted the time study, and are armed with pages of information and notes, let's see what you have learned. Group your activities into logical groupings: administrative duties, meetings, appointments, routine tasks, nonroutine tasks, and so forth.

Now see what you can learn. Are you surprised at some of the time? Does it seem excessive? Take a look at your notes for those areas. What can you learn about what causes the use

> ### Assignment
>
> For every area you define as a problem, start looking for ways to fix the problem. Sections of this book will help.

of time? Are there things you can control? Are there areas you can make changes that might reduce the amount of time you spend on that area?

What you will find are places where some simple changes, many outlined in this book, will make major differences in total time spent on tasks. You cannot fix anything until you know where to look. Now you do.

> ### Epilogue
>
> *Everyone has places and activities that use more time than they should. We just don't know where they are or what they are. This process leads to solutions.*

4

Establish Clear Goals for Your Job

As you look at your job, one of the things you need to figure out is what you expect of that job in light of your career. As we all now know, we will not spend our lives in any one job. Probably not even in one company. Perhaps not even in one career field! At least, that's what the Department of Labor statistics are currently telling us.

So what is it that you expect from this job? Set some goals for your own personal and professional growth. These goals should be made in light of your long-range aspirations. These goals should logically help lead to the accomplishment of those long-range aspirations.

If your long-range goal is to be a senior officer of public relations and communications in a major company, then what do you need to accomplish to get there?

- You need a degree in public relations.

- You need professional association membership.

- You need professional certification.

- You need a graduate degree.

- You will need progressive jobs in public relations in a number of sectors over a 20-year period with increasing responsibilities.

- You may need an industry specialization.

With these goals in mind, what objectives should you set for your current job? Look at that "progressive jobs" and "increasing responsibilities" stuff. Can you get that from this job? Then establish those as objectives. Do you need to start preparing for professional certification? Then set an objective and set aside time.

You should establish clear objectives that you want to accomplish for every job you will ever hold. Then work to accomplish those objectives. Plan your job activities, and your time, accordingly.

Assignment

Set career and job goals. Your own goals and objectives, not your boss's or your company's. Then work to achieve those goals and objectives within the context of your current job.

Epilogue

If we don't have goals and objectives, we simply wander through life aimlessly. And aimless is likely to lead somewhere we don't want to end up.

5

Write Down Your Goals and Objectives

It is not enough to just establish some career goals and job objectives. You need to write them down and refer to them routinely. I went through this process many years ago at the urging of my then-boss. I can't thank him enough now for putting me through that exercise.

But I wrote down those goals and objectives in clear language and have referred to them routinely ever since. No, they have not stayed exactly the same. Some of the goals have been modified, and, of course, I created new objectives for every job I ever held.

Assignment

Write down your career and life goals and the objectives you have for your current job. Keep them somewhere you can refer to on a routine, perhaps monthly, basis. Keep updating them as you move from job to job.

But because I wrote them down, I have a clear record 25 years later of how I came to be on the road I am on today. Writing them down also gave me a life document to refer to when faced with major career and life decisions, such as when to change jobs, or when to consider certain activities at certain times.

These written records I still have in the original notebook I first used to create them. They are valuable life tools.

Epilogue

Written records allow you to do some decision-making about your jobs and your career—sometimes even your life. And they help you know what you want from every job and what kind of time you should spend on those personal objectives in each job.

6

Set Clear Goals for Time Use

Armed with your life and career goals, and your job objectives, you can now begin to create some expectation of the time you should spend on them. Look over your job objectives and allocate time every week or month for achieving these objectives.

This also helps you make decisions about which additional duties you might take on and which activities you take on after work, or in addition to your work.

For example, one of my goals was to become involved in a professional association of my peers. A couple of jobs ago, I set a job objective to do just that. And I established time every month to be involved in that association. It helped me orient my time both on the job and after the job to my long-range career goals.

A very useful device.

Assignment

Using your job objectives for your current job, establish some time for achieving those objectives. It might be time during the workday, or time after work, or time from both areas. But establish how you plan to use your time to get these objectives accomplished.

Epilogue

Not only will this process help you achieve your life and career goals, but it will also help you orient yourself to the job and plan for the time you use on the job.

7

Set Daily and Weekly Objectives

With these time allocations, establish some daily and weekly objectives that involve time working to achieve them. Your weekly objectives might be quite modest, but, taken over weeks and months, they will add up and lead to achieving those job objectives and lead to meeting career goals.

The key point here is planning to allocate time to spend on the key things in your life. This can, and often should, include personal goals and objectives that involve family. Don't forget your obligations to them.

Assignment

Establish some overall time objectives each day and week to spend on achieving your job objectives. This will make certain you will get to those goals you set for your life and career.

Epilogue

Planning for your future and for your success is the name of the game here. If you set aside time, you'll get there. If you only use time for these things as it comes available, you'll find yourself out of time every time and you'll never get there.

8

Start Your Day the Night Before

The best way to get off to a good start in the morning is to do it the night before!

Yes. Prepare for your day the night before by doing some simple things that will help you begin your day efficiently and effectively. It's a simple thing to do.

First, at the end of each day prior to leaving for home, review your schedule for the next day. Determine the major activities and tasks you will be accomplishing the next day and do any preparation that might be appropriate: retrieve the necessary files, send any coordinating messages, read any materials you need to consume in preparation.

Assignment

Start your day the night before by making any preparations you need to then. You'll begin your day fresh and prepared, not behind the schedule already.

The idea is to make all your preparations for the next day the night before. Then, when you walk in you are ready to start, effectively, efficiently, and with no delays for preparation. Your preparation is already done.

Epilogue

This technique has the added advantage of preparing you psychologically for the day and giving your day a great start.

9

Don't Procrastinate

I'll write more about this later in the book, but one of the most time-consuming and time-challenging problems many people face is procrastination.

Procrastination is putting things off instead of doing them right away. It's waiting until the last minute to complete a task or project because it isn't exciting or isn't interesting. Or perhaps it's just a project that you arenot prepared for, don't know enough about, or is threatening in some way.

> ## Assignment
>
> Do some self-analysis. Determine if you are a procrastinator. If so, stop. If you need help, pay particular attention to Ideas 115–123 of this book.

Though not terribly damaging in the big picture of things, some studies have shown procrastination to cost a person twice as much time as the task should take.

Start thinking about this now. Are you one of those people? Do you put things off until the last minute? If so, you are costing yourself lots of time, and managing your time badly.

> ### Epilogue
> *Procrastination is terribly costly in time and efficiency. It's one of the most significant causes of lost time and overtime.*

10

Pareto's Principle: 80–20

Okay, so who's this Pareto guy and why do we care?

Vilfredo Pareto was an Italian economist. He observed that, in any give endeavor, 80 percent of the rewards we receive come from only 20 percent of the effort. He's telling

> ### *Assignment*
>
> As you think about prioritizing your work, as you will in the next few ideas, remember Pareto's Principle.

us that only 20 percent of the work we do will lead us to most of the rewards in life.

That's pretty depressing! We will be rewarded for only 20 percent of the work we do? Well, not quite, but most of our reward does come from a very small percentage of our work. So what does it mean to us? How do we use this information?

Knowing this allows us to prioritize our work appropriately. We will want to put the things that we believe will bring us the proper rewards—personal, professional, organizational—high on our priority list and everything else lower.

Epilogue

Let's face it: though it all needs to get done, the stuff that we are rewarded for should be the most important stuff we do and should get priority for our attention.

11

The ABCs of Prioritizing

The first step in getting control of your time management is to prioritize your work. If we put the stuff that brings us reward first, how do we organize this?

It's not brain surgery, but there is a simple system to help. The system just asks you to organize all your work into three categories, from high to low priority. We'll call them Category A, B, and C. A is high priority, B is medium priority, and C is low priority.

Now go ahead and set up your prioritization system and do this routinely. The next few ideas will walk you through what fits in each category.

> ### *Assignment*
>
> Regularly prioritize your tasks, especially when you make up your To Do List. Use this ABC system.

> ### Epilogue
>
> *Not everything is high priority. Not everything is really important. And not everything has to be done today. This system allows you to organize effectively around the things that are important.*

12

The A in ABC

The priority items are the must do's. These are things that meet some or all of the following criteria:

- ◆ Not doing them will get you fired.

- ◆ Doing them fit the 20-percent rule of Pareto's Principle.

- ◆ They are things that have a due date near today.

- They are things that match your personal and professional goals or objectives.

- They are assigned by the boss.

Your criteria might be different, but there will be criteria that will dictate that some things need to be done NOW. That is your A List. Things that take priority over everything else. Things that are important. Things that have consequences.

> **Assignment**
>
> Prioritize your tasks and duties. Decide which are A priority and put them at the top of your To Do List. Manage them closely and get them done. They are important.

Epilogue

Use your To Do List to manage these items. Remember, if it's on the A List, it's important to someone important. That might be you or it might be your boss. It doesn't matter. Just don't make everything an A List item. Then the system has no value.

13

The B *in ABC*

The B priorities are things that need to be done but are not necessarily of major consequence or not due soon. Examine your tasks and organize the B List. It should be a group of tasks that need to get completed but either are not important enough to get done today or tomorrow, or simply don't need to get done soon. Perhaps they don't need to get done until a week from now.

Put your B List on your To Do List below the A List items. But don't think you can forget about these tasks. Many will simply move up into the A List over time as their due dates get closer.

Assignment

Look at your remaining tasks after the A List is determined. Cull out those things that simply aren't due yet or have lesser consequences. They may not provide the potential for reward or there's some other reason why they are not as important as A List items, but they still need to be accomplished. Get those B items on your To Do List.

So as you have time, work on some B List items along with the A List. That's why they go on your To Do List in the first place: to be managed and fit in when you can.

Epilogue

Never forget that B List items still have to be done. They just don't necessarily need to be done today. But perhaps tomorrow....

14

The C in ABC

Now to that C List. But first, a story.

Earlier in my career I had a friend who used the ABC system. He always put his A List in a basket on his desk to be worked on immediately. His B List items he had in another basket below the A List basket. But his C List, now that was a different story. He put all his C List work in the bottom drawer of his desk. And he never brought it out unless someone asked about it.

You see, his C List was comprised of items that simply were not important to him or anyone he cared about. They often died in the bottom drawer. If someone came in and asked him about one of those items, he would pull it out and it would become part of the B List. Otherwise, that was where work went to die for him.

And that's a pretty good way to look at your C List. It's stuff that just isn't that important. Stuff that isn't critical. Stuff that has no potential for rewards. Stuff no one is likely to care about. We all get that stuff. Put it in the C List and do it if you have time; ignore it otherwise. If its status changes, you can always move it up to the B List.

Assignment

Take those items that are not important and put them on the C List. Put them away somewhere and review them occasionally to see if any should move up. If you have extra time (ha!), go ahead and work on some of them. Otherwise, let them age as good wine does.

Epilogue

Do remember to occasionally review your C List. Sometimes projects and tasks have to be moved up for a variety of reasons. Something that was unimportant today might suddenly turn out to be important next week. Otherwise, in your crowded schedule, concentrate on the stuff that matters.

15

Write Down Tasks as You Receive Them

We often get instructions and tasks passed to us verbally. Though not always the best way to do this, it's certainly the most common. Unfortunately, in the heat of the daily battle, sometimes these things can be forgotten.

It's always a good policy to immediately make a note about any task given to you verbally. This begins your work record for the task or project and allows you to have a document to remind you of it. It should be written as soon as possible after it is given so the memory of the instructions is fresh and you can capture all the detail you were provided.

It should also immediately go on your prioritized To Do List. Put it where it

Assignment

Write down verbal instructions and new tasks communicated verbally. This starts your record, gets it on to your To Do List, and allows you to track your task to success.

belongs, but get it on there. That way you will not forget it as your review your To Do List every day.

Epilogue

Capturing this information in writing saves you time later in remembering the task late and having to scramble to get it done. It also saves you with all the details so you don't have to waste time going back for information you were already provided.

16

Set Deadlines for Assignments

All of your assignments and everything on your To Do List should have a deadline for completion. This deadline should be one you impose yourself and should be a day or so before the actual deadline.

Assignment

Assign deadlines for every task and project. Make them one or two days in advance of the actual deadline to provide yourself with a buffer in case of problems.

Setting deadlines provides you with a planning and organizing tool, and setting deadlines early allows for problems or slippage in your work schedule while still allowing the work to get done on time. So, if you are out sick a couple of days and one of your project's deadline is the day you return, you don't have to scramble to get it done, because you have built in some buffer time between your deadline and the actual deadline.

Epilogue

I use this method routinely, and I find that my bacon has been saved many times without burning the midnight oil by having deadlines and, more importantly, setting deadlines early.

17

Under-Commit and Over-Deliver

One of the pitfalls of all work is the danger of over-committing yourself to work. Later I'll write about the ability to say NO, but this is a danger we all face constantly. You need to be able to keep your commitments, both professional and personal, at a level that allows you some ability to easily adjust to changing conditions and changing priorities.

Assignment

Fence part of every day for contingencies and for other unpredicted work. It will require you to be tough with decision-making, and you will have to develop the ability to say no or say "later."

This means that sometimes you have to say no to people. It means that you might have to delegate some work. It means that you need to protect about 20 percent of your time to use to handle the many things that just come up and cannot be planned for. Yet you can plan for them if you keep yourself only 80 percent committed.

Just as importantly, you need to give more than 100 percent on every task or project. That's what leads both to job satisfaction as well as supervisor satisfaction. Don't just do the job—do it right, on time, and better than anyone else. That kind of behavior brings rewards.

Epilogue

Obviously you cannot say no to your boss. But you can say no to someone who asks you to serve on a committee, or someone who asks you to help coach the office softball team after work. Protect 20 percent of your time and you'll save time later.

18

Keep Score

We all keep score. Let's admit it. Of course we do. Keeping score is the American way! And it's not a bad thing to do on the job as well.

But by keeping score on the job, I don't mean you versus everyone else. I mean keep score against the To Do List—against all

Assignment

As you complete tasks and projects, check them off your To Do List visibly. Use a special color to annotate tasks that are completed. The To Do List will start to resemble a score card and you'll get motivated by it.

those tasks that you have to accomplish. On your To Do List, check them off boldly as you go. I use a red line to do that. It stands out.

As I see things getting done by red lines appearing on my list, I am keeping score. I'm tracking my success. And I keep doing that every day. It's almost a personal reward system to see how I'm doing against the other team—that is, the items on the list. It's actually quite motivating and keeps me on task and on target.

Epilogue

I've had others try this trick in other offices I've worked in. And although it doesn't always work (because some people are simply not competitive), it works quite effectively for most people. It keeps them on task and actually makes them more efficient. And, yes, they save time.

19

Make a To Do List

Managing your time means knowing what to do with your time. Although it seems an inconvenience, creating a To Do List is a great tool for making the most of the time available to you. Once I started using a To Do List, I became much better at managing my time—and I saved time as well!

A To Do List is simply that: a list of things that must be done. The list keeps you aware of the tasks you need to accomplish and provides you with a tool to manage those tasks. To make the best use of a To Do List, follow these simple procedures:

1. List all tasks that have to be accomplished.
2. Then order them by date of requirement (when the task must be accomplished).
3. Check off items that are completed.
4. Update routinely (once a day should do).

The To Do List should be your primary task management tool. As such, you should refer to it routinely. Use it. Manage it. Update it as new tasks come in and as you complete old tasks.

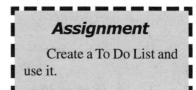

Assignment

Create a To Do List and use it.

Some software programs allow you to create and manage Task Lists or To Do Lists. If you are comfortable using these programs, then do so. If not, just use a lined piece of paper. Remake it once a week or so.

Epilogue

Using a To Do List will help you prioritize your work, be more efficient, and save you time.

20

Use the To Do List!

I already said that, I know. But I didn't tell you how. Here's my story; steal any good ideas from it.

Every evening before I go home I review my To Do List. I reprioritize anything due the next day by moving it to the top of the list so I'll see it first thing in the morning. I reprioritize anything else according to when it is due.

Every morning, I review my To Do List and set my day's work accordingly. As new tasks come in that I am responsible for, I add them to the list in the right order of priority. As you can imagine, those things due soon are at the top of the list, and those due later are at the bottom.

This is not foolproof. I often will put something toward the top that requires a great deal of work so I get to it soon enough to have the project done on time. In addition, anything that is really important to me or the organization might end up higher on the list than the due date suggests.

> **Assignment**
>
> Start using your To Do List on a daily basis to manage your workload and your time.

As tasks are accomplished, I cross them off the list. At the end of the day I review and…well, you know.

> **Epilogue**
>
> *I have found that using a To Do List saves me time and makes certain that I don't have to "burn the midnight oil" because I forgot something.*

21

Share the To Do List

Because my To Do List is electronic, I share that with the other members of my work team and my boss. It helps when the boss is determining who is to take on new projects or tasks to review others to see what their workload is. My boss can quickly look at my To Do List and see if I can handle another project or task.

Members of my work team can do the same when they are looking to get help on a project or pass on some work. Everyone knows what I'm working on and can adjust accordingly. If you don't use an electronic list everyone can see, simply post yours outside your door or cubicle.

> ### *Assignment*
>
> Make your To Do List available to others in your office, and especially to your boss. This helps communicate your workload to others so they don't gang up on you.

Of course, if you don't have much to do, expect some work to come your way!

Epilogue

This will save you from project or task overload, hopefully, and can also help communicate all the tasks you are working on to your boss. Of course, to be useful, it has to be accurate and up to date.

22

Update the To Do List

The To Do List is worthless if it is not up to date—worthless to you and worthless to others. If the list is out of date, you can't trust it to tell you where your priorities lay. As a result, you could easily spend time on a project or task at the expense of something due very soon, then spend evening hours catching up when you discover the error.

Also, you need to update the list as you go so that, as projects change and deadlines get moved, you annotate that on your list and adjust the items on the priority list.

Of course, always check off items that have been accomplished. It's a great way to track what you have done on a given day or during a given week.

Finally, make sure you add all new tasks and get them in the priority list. When you start relying on this list, missing just one item can cause you no end of headaches later.

And if it's up to date, your boss will see how you are managing time and work, and may pass on new work and tasks to others—or relieve you of some of your workload if you appear to be overloaded. When I did a

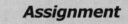

Assignment

Keep your To Do List scrupulously up to date. And provide a copy to your boss.

manual To Do List (pen and paper) I always provided a copy to my boss every Monday morning so he knew what I was working on.

> **Epilogue**
>
> *At first my boss wasn't sure why I was giving him the list. After about two weeks he found it so valuable that he started requiring it of everyone who worked for him. Keep your To Do List scrupulously up to date. And provide a copy to your boss.*

23

Organize Your Workspace: General

You've all seen those signs over people's desks: "A cluttered desk is a brilliant mind." Well, maybe. But that's similar to those signs in kitchens that read: "Never eat food cooked by a skinny chef." Nonsense.

But usually a cluttered desk means it's managed by a cluttered mind, and a mind that is not as productive as it could be. Your time is often controlled by how well you control your environment.

> **Assignment**
>
> Examine your work space to determine if it is organized to allow you to win the war. If not, reorganize. Follow some of the simple ideas that follow.

Your workspace is your castle! At least while you are at work. And your castle should be organized in such a way as to allow you to be as productive and efficient as possible.

So think about how you work, and examine your office or cubicle. Is it orderly? Is it organized to allow you to work efficiently? Does it help you control the flow of work, or paper, or visitors? If not, you need think about an office makeover. Makeovers are very popular now, so give it a go.

Epilogue

Organization leads to efficiency. Efficiency leads to saved time. Save time by being efficient. Be efficient by being organized. Start with your workspace.

24

Organize Your Workspace: The Desktop

The first problem area I usually find when I help people get organized is the desktop. If I find piles of paper in no seeming order all over the desktop, I know I have my work cut out for me. Organizing is fairly simple, but is also fairly personal. There is no one

Assignment

Take a look at your desktop organization. Is everything stacked up haphazardly? Disorganized? Spread out all over the place? Get organized! Conduct a makeover of your desktop.

way or right answer. Only you can decide the best way to organize your desktop.

However, there are some principles that you should consider. They are:

- ◆ How does work come to you? By paper, by e-mail, or by mail? Is there a central location on your desk where such new assignments can live until you handle them? If not, create one. The traditional "in basket" is still a useful tool today.

- ◆ How do you manage the documents for a task or project? Are then stacked up in a pile somewhere? Do you know where? Organizing these documents, even notes from meetings, is important. The easiest way is the traditional manila folder. Put the folder in a file or in a wire rack on your desktop.

- ◆ Where are your tools (pencils, pens, the telephone, the computer, office supplies, and so forth)? If they are scattered about haphazardly, then organize them. Have the computer where you can reach it easily. Put the phone at hand, not behind you. Keep office supplies in a drawer somewhere, easy to reach but out of the way. Pens, pencils, and notepads should not be strewn about the desk, but in a drawer at easy reach.

Epilogue

Organization saves time. And time is what we are after.

25

Organize Your Workspace: Paper Files

Those who said the computer would lead us to the paperless office were lying! There's more paper than ever. So, what to do with all that paper.

All too often, it ends up in piles on the desk. This leads to lost time while you look for just the right document or file or report. Not only do you waste your time, but you tend to waste others' time as well as they wait for you on the phone or in the office.

Again, the best solution is the traditional one: the ubiquitous manila folder. Put all documents into a common folder. Organize them in any way you want. Chronological works if you date all your files. Or you might want to attach the project

Assignment

Organize your paper files. Use manila folders and establish a system that works for you.

or task time line on the inside cover and organize the papers inside by content. Whatever works for you is the best way to do it.

Epilogue

Getting all your paper into folders creates order from chaos and productivity from waste, and will truly save you time during each and every day.

26

Organize Your Workspace: Folders

Okay, so what do you do with all those folders you've just made? Stack them back on the desk? I think not! Create a filing system instead.

There are lots of books out there that tell you how to organize your files. Ignore them all! Organize them any way you want so long as you know what the system is and where the files can be found. That's all that matters.

> ### Assignment
>
> This system is simple and easy to set up and use. Try it. You'll find it, or something similar to it, a real time-saver.

My method is to keep active folders for working projects on my desk on wire racks where I can easily reach them. I store older files in a filing cabinet. My system for the filing cabinet? Simple: alphabetical. No muss, no fuss. Project name by alpha order. It's easy even for someone else to find if I'm out of the office.

> ### Epilogue
>
> *You will find yourself much more productive using a filing system. Nothing fancy, but any system has been demonstrated to save up to 15 minutes a day compared to those with no system.*

Organize Your Workspace: Electronic Files

But the paper files are not the only files we have today. All those computer records, reports, memos, e-mails, and so forth need to go somewhere too.

Again, set up folders for them all and name the electronic folders the same way and with the same labels you used for paper folders.

Assignment

Set up folders and files for your tasks and projects. Put the current ones on your electronic desktop for quick retrieval.

I always find that it is helpful to keep current task and project folders right on the desktop so I don't have to search for them or take three or four clicks to reach them. One click opens the folder and the list of documents.

Also remember to clearly label the various documents in the folder so you can tell what is in the document. Nothing wastes time as much time as having to open three or four documents until you find the right one just because your labels were sloppy.

Epilogue

You'll save an enormous amount of time doing this. Once I got the handle on this system, I suspect I've saved about 15 minutes a day over my old haphazard system. Again, remember: A little here and a little there, and you've saved a significant amount of time.

28

Organize Your Workspace: Contacts

You have to call people all the time. You send mail all the time. You address memos and letters all the time. So you need a quick way to reach your contacts or their information.

The old system, one I grew up on, was to keep an address book. Yes, a paper address book with little colored tabs and everything. And it worked fine. The only weakness was that it is a written record, not an electronic one.

> **Assignment**
>
> Establish your electronic address book. Pick an application and use it. Once you spend the time to set it up initially, it will save you time daily as you need that information. Just remember to keep it up to date.

Today I am much more efficient because I keep all that information in an electronic database. I use a common product, and there are a number of very good ones out there, including Microsoft Outlook, ACT, and Goldmine to name just a few.

The advantage to all of these products is that they are electronic. You can export information quickly from them into word processing documents, onto labels, and into databases and spreadsheets. And you can look things up very quickly. Paper is slow compared to these electronic address books.

And, if you use a PDA (personal data assistant), you can synchronize your data right to the PDA from your computer and have all that data at hand when you are out of the office. Now that's time-saving efficiency.

Epilogue

The combination of the electronic address book and a PDA has been one of the most important time-saving tools of the past decade. You should take advantage, as many others have.

29

Organize Your Workspace: Cull Your Files

Sometimes they just get away from you. Those old files build up fast. So fast you suddenly run out of room to store them. What to do?

Get rid of them. I have a colleague who works at a consulting firm. The firm produces a lot of paper, including memos, research documents, draft reports, and so on. She indicates that they have one day each month where everyone in the firm goes through their files and cleans them out. She says they have to be ruthless about it!

They keep anything that has long-term value: samples for future work, final reports, basic research documents. But they toss anything that was used to create those final documents: old memos (their rule is older than three

Assignment

Don't let your files overwhelm you. Cull and kill on a routine basis—perhaps once a month or quarterly.

47

years), personal notes of meetings and calls, the survey returns from research or interview records from old interviews. All that goes.

Their goal is to keep from having to store anything in long-term storage, but retain anything that would be of lasting value. To protect their clients, everything is shredded.

Epilogue

Old records just make it hard to find the valuable stuff, and it takes your time to wade through it all. Don't destroy records you are legally bound to keep, such as financial records and personnel records.

30

Handle Your Mail Efficiently

Some people just wait all day for the mail and distribution to arrive. It's the highlight of their day. Unfortunately, they often end up anticipating it, and when it arrives just have to jump on it immediately no matter what they are doing.

Unfortunately, both of these behaviors are time-wasters.

Assignment

Mail and internal distribution usually happens around the same time or times every day in most organizations. Set your schedule to get it and handle it. Do that around your other projects; don't let this stuff interrupt your thinking and working processes.

The best way to handle mail and internal distribution is to just let it arrive when it arrives, and set a time to handle it. Don't let it drive your schedule; you keep control. All too often I see people stop something important or interrupt a project to open their mail and look at internal distribution.

This leads to lost time, as they then have their day fragmented by that activity. They have to return to that project and get back into it before they are as effective as they were when they were engrossed in it. It costs time.

Epilogue

Every time you let something or someone break into your flow of work, you lose time. Don't let this happen to you.

31

Use a Suspense File

One time-killer, and one that causes late nights and much worry, is forgetting a key deadline. Ever happen to you? Of course. You discover at 3 o'clock in the afternoon that you have forgotten to create a report to be used at a meeting the next morning. What happens? You work late to get it done, and that sets you back on other projects you'll have to catch up on the next day.

The way to keep this from happening is to establish a "suspense file." This is a simple set of files numbered from 1 to 31. These represent the days of each month (yes, I know, not every month has 31 days, but...). Into each file folder (yep, those

> **Assignment**
>
> Create a suspense file for yourself and check it every day. Remember that it will not work for you unless you use it regularly.

pesky manila folders) put any document or a note of an action that is due the next day. For example, if you have a report due on Friday the 10th, in the file folder for the 9th put a reminder document or the original task document. Then, each morning, check your suspense file.

This system keeps you from being surprised and helps you organize your work time. Of course, if something is going to take longer to accomplish, put that item a few days earlier in the file folder.

> **Epilogue**
>
> *This one simple trick has reduced the amount of hours I have had to spend doing things at the last minute to a bare minimum. And as a consequence, it has saved many hours of late nights.*

32

Keep Only One Planner/Scheduler

You absolutely need to have command of your schedule. And the only way to do that is to keep a calendar or scheduler for all the activities you are involved in and are scheduled to participate in. Keep it as detailed as you can.

There are a number of excellent computer applications that will help you with this, or you can simply create one with paper forms. This allows you to refer to it routinely to make certain you are on time to meetings and appointments.

You can also use one of these to track your deadlines. Just add them to the schedule each day as notes. Then your suspense file and your scheduler both help you stay on target to get everything done on time.

A reminder, though: keep only one of these. Don't try to have one in your computer and another one in a small pocket calendar. Not only is this duplication of effort, but it is almost certain you will forget to update one or the other and will miss something. You could, however, use a PDA.

Assignment

Create a daily planner/scheduler for yourself that includes all your tasks for each day and any meetings or appointments.

Epilogue

How does this save time? It keeps you from missing something and having to take extra time to make up for it.

33

What to Keep—and What Not to Keep

Some people just can't do without their "stuff." Their office/cubicle is just packed full of their stuff. Know anyone like that? I have a friend who simply cannot throw anything away. As a result, his office is completely cluttered with all his "stuff."

Ordinarily this would not be much of a problem, but when too much stuff accumulates, you begin to lose track of where everything is. It leads to sloppy filing, sloppy record-keeping, and an inability to keep control of your work environment. So, when someone requests something from my friend, he has it—and knows he has it—he just has to search for it every time. So it costs extra time.

> **Assignment**
>
> Inventory your workspace. Organize. Get rid of that old stuff. Store the stuff you use. Put everything else you just think you might need somewhere out of the way. Keep your workspace clear and ready for action.

Guard against this loss of time by getting rid of all that "stuff." If you don't need it, get rid of it. If you do need it, put it in a routine place you can find it easily. If you "might" need it, store it away somewhere where you can get at it when you need it, but somewhere that doesn't clutter your work environment.

> ### Epilogue
>
> *Don't waste time trying to find things. Put everything in its right place and store away things that will cost you time working around later.*

34

What to Do With Draft Documents

We all have those documents we write that are drafts. We pass them around for others to review; get their comments, red marks, and corrections; and then compile a final document for use.

> ### *Assignment*
>
> Start today with a new policy of disposing of draft documents. Shred them after the final version is used or approved.

What do we do with all those drafts we now have? Most of us file them forever! Why? They are no good to anyone. So the answer is to pitch that stuff!

Draft documents should be kept only as long as the final document has not been used or approved. Once that happens, all those drafts should be shredded and disposed of. There is absolutely no reason to keep that stuff around junking up files.

Epilogue

There is only one reason to keep any draft documents: CYA. If you need that, keep them only until that need is gone.

35

Handle Business Cards

We all give them out, and we all get them all the time. Business cards from people we meet and do business with—or not. I have stacks of them in my office. Every time I go somewhere I tend to meet new people. And we always exchange business cards.

It's a useful convention in our society. But those business cards can sure build up. There are a couple of ways to handle all those cards so they can be useful. Certainly just keeping them in a desk drawer is not the right answer.

One way, perhaps the best way, is to simply make a point of transferring the data from the business card to a contact database once you return to the office. That's what I do routinely. Because I write notes on the backs of the card—the place I met the person, circumstances, personal observations—I also transfer that information to the database. Then I pitch the card. It's served its usefulness, and I don't need a bunch of cards hanging around cluttering my workspace.

> ### *Assignment*
>
> Pick a solution and use it. The best way is the database, especially a contact database.

Another way is to buy card notebooks. These are small-sized binders with inserts for business cards. Though not as useful as a database, these offer a neat way to maintain those cards, and their information, for future use.

Find a method of filing them that makes sense to you. Just don't let them pile up. Because when you need one, you will then have to waste time searching for it.

Epilogue

I've watched friends who simply toss their cards in a side desk drawer search through that drawer for the card from someone they suddenly want to call or contact. What a waste of time! A little organization goes a long way.

36

Know Your Best Working Hours

Scheduling is important to creating an efficient workday. Scheduling, although considered restrictive by some, is the best tool in our arsenal to combat wasted and lost time.

One of the first things you need to understand about yourself, however, is your most effective working hours. We all have them, and they tend to be different for everyone. I, for example, am a morning person. I rise every day at 5 a.m. and am at work by 7 a.m. I am very efficient and task-oriented in the morning hours. An analysis of my productivity showed me that I actually get 65 percent of my day's work done in the first four to five hours of the day.

You might be different. You might be an evening person or an afternoon person. Whichever you are, plan your day accordingly.

If you are a morning person, put your most important task early on your schedule. If you are an afternoon person, put them

Assignment

Be a little introspective and determine what your best and most efficient working hours are. Then schedule your most important work for that time of day.

in the afternoon. Know when you are at your most efficient, and use that knowledge in getting the most out of your day.

Epilogue

This doesn't mean you ignore the rest of the day! It just means that you acknowledge when you are at your best and take advantage of that. It simply makes the best use of your time.

37

Make Critical Appointments at Your Best Times

One of the things you want to do with your best working times is schedule important appointments and meetings when you are at your best and most efficient. If you are a morning person, as I am, schedule important meetings, appointments, and office calls for the morning. I find I'm more efficient and use time better that way.

Assignment

Schedule meetings, appointments, and office calls during your peak working times, when you are at your best. Though this is not always possible, focus on getting most of them in when you are most efficient.

I'm also sharper then and do better work during the mornings. Things don't take as long and the outcomes are better.

Scheduling these events later in the day for me leads to longer meetings and longer appointments because I'm not at my sharpest. You'll find the same thing happening to you.

So, once you know what your best working times, conduct your important meetings then. You'll find you have shorter meetings with better outcomes when you schedule this way.

Epilogue

I timed meetings I called. Those that were held in the afternoon always went 15–20 minutes longer than those in the morning—even if it was the same group on the same topic! Strategic scheduling of meetings does save time.

38

Group Similar Tasks

Once you are on a roll with one kind of task, you are focused on the elements and the type of work required for that task. So, it only makes sense that if you schedule similar tasks together, you will be more focused and less fragmented. You'll find that you can be much more efficient if you group all your like tasks together at one time.

Assignment

Group similar tasks together during the day or week. You'll be more efficient and use your time better. Your outcomes will also be better because you'll be focused in your work.

For example, I group all my administrative tasks together at one time of the day—sometimes one time each week. I hate doing this stuff, so I group it all together so that when I do focus on it, I can get it done as quickly as possible.

I found that when I scattered these tasks throughout the day or week, I was not nearly as efficient with time. It tended to fragment the day and cost time. With my way, I also get a series of unpleasant tasks out of the way all at once.

Epilogue

Once I discovered the efficiencies of doing administrative tasks all together, I looked at other tasks I could group together for efficiency. I found four more areas I could do with this. It has saved me significant time every week.

39

Put Up a Fence

When we fence our yards, it is either to keep something in—a pet, for example—or to keep something out—such as someone else's pet. Or kids. We need to do this with our work schedule, too.

Once you know your most effective time of the day, put up a fence. Fence the time to keep others out.

Assignment

When you plan your day—as you must (see the next few ideas on scheduling)—make certain you fence your most efficient times. Protect them and you'll be much more productive and go home on time.

The more you keep them out, the more you can concentrate on your work during your most effective time of the day without getting fragmented and interrupted.

How to do that? Some tricks: If you share electronic calendars, block the time out. If you have a door, close it. If you get interrupted, be polite but dismissive. Send them away with an appointment for later. Put your phone on DND (do not disturb). Don't check your e-mail (and stop the system from popping up with that "you have mail" message!).

Epilogue

Fencing that time keeps you in and minimizes the distractions and interruptions—and thus makes the best use of your time.

40

Block Contingency Time Every Day

Stuff happens! We all know that. Almost every day things occur that you have not planned for you yet must be dealt with. These unplanned activities can certainly eat away at a day, especially if you don't plan for them.

What can happen? Your boss stops by with a new assignment and eats up a half hour. A client calls for a long chat about a future project she wants you to work on—and eats up 45 minutes. An employee has a personal problem and just needs someone to listen and perhaps make some suggestions—another 25 minutes. One of your work teams experiences a delay in a project and you have to step in to help make a series of new decisions— 40 minutes gone.

They happen and you can't stop them. So, plan for the unexpected.

> ### Assignment
>
> Every day, set aside some time for unplanned activities. Only you know how much time to assign based on your experience, but always plan for the unexpected.

> ### Epilogue
>
> *I have a friend who did a detailed analysis of how much time during his day was spent on unplanned activities. He was shocked. He was spending more than two hours a day on unplanned activities. Yet he had not scheduled any such time, so he was spending an extra two hours each evening catching up. Now he plans for it.*

41

Scheduling: A 5-Step Process

Scheduling is a process. And there a lot of people out there who can suggest a way to effectively schedule your daily work. Here's one that is at least as good as anything else you will find.

Assignment

Start tonight. Create a work schedule for tomorrow and stick to it.

Keep a schedule for every workday. Conduct your planning for each day the night before so you are ready for each day when you arrive. The best tool is an electronic calendar, but you can use a simple paper calendar if you don't use a computer. The main point is to plan your day. It doesn't really matter what tool you use to do it.

This process has five easy steps, takes very little time, will saves you time, and allows you to be more efficient.

Epilogue

Use this five-step process. It will save you time in the long run and does not take a lot of time itself.

42

Scheduling: Step 1

The first step is to clearly identify the time you have available. This means knowing what meetings you have to block out, what out-of-office events will take place that will keep you from working, and so on.

Assignment

Identify your time available. Block out things that will limit your productive work time, such as meetings.

Remember, too, to account for those things in your personal life, such as the kids' soccer match, or your daughter's piano recital that evening. These personal things will be identified during your goal-planning session we discussed earlier in the book, so don't forget them.

Once all these things are identified, put this time in your calendar as available. Then move to Step 2.

Epilogue

Don't discount this step in the process. You have times you are not available. Block them out so you can plan effectively.

43

Scheduling: Step 2

Now that you know what time is available each day, determine the priority tasks that must be accomplished that day for you to be able to declare the day a success. Block time to accomplish those tasks and list those first on your day's To Do List.

Don't forget the To Do List as a part of this process. The list must match the calendar.

Assignment

Identify your "must do" tasks and estimate the time required for them. Then block that time on your calendar.

Epilogue

These tasks are the important ones that, if accomplished, make the day a success. Do this for every day and in the time alloted, and every day will be a success.

44

Scheduling: Step 3

The third step is to plan for the regular housekeeping tasks you have to accomplish every day or every week. You know these things—those administrative tasks I wrote about earlier, or that standard report task that you

Assignment

Mark your calendar for those housekeeping tasks and functions you know about so they always get done on time.

have to do every Friday. Often these will be recurring and you can put them in your calendar quite quickly.

Epilogue

These things take time, but if you plan for them routinely, they will take the minimum time necessary and not be an afterthought that makes you stay a half hour late every day.

45

Scheduling: Step 4

During Step 4 you block some of that contingency time we discussed in Idea #40. Literally block time for such things. They will not happen when you schedule them, but you'll be glad you accounted for the time later when they do happen.

In using your schedule, you just move things around each day to reflect reality. But if you don't block this time initially, it's not there to move around and you end up working late. Again.

> ### *Assignment*
> Block some time now for contingencies and emergencies.

> ### Epilogue
> *Only you know how much based on your experience, but always put in some time every day for this. You'll need it.*

46

Scheduling: Step 5

You are almost there. And none of this should have taken very much time at all.

Now plan for some time for you to work on personal and professional goals. This might be time for reading. Or time for some research. Or time for taking an online course. Or time for…well, you get my drift. This is YOUR time to get better at being who you want to be. It's based on those personal and professional goals discussed earlier in this book.

> ### *Assignment*
>
> Now, finally, complete your schedule with some personal/professional time just for you. No time left? Make some!

How much time you have left for this kind of activity will depend on what you have accomplished in the first four steps. If you have NO time left for this, make some adjustments to your schedule. You should have at least a little time every day of your life for these activities. And the only way to make that happen is to build in some time in your schedule for them.

> #### Epilogue
>
> *This is Step 5, but it is just as important as the others. Don't forget this step, and don't just write it off as not possible today. Because you'll do that tomorrow, too. And the next day. And before you know it, you are planning no time for yourself. Don't let this happen.*

47

Use an Electronic Calendar

One way to maximize your schedule is to put it in an electronic calendar. I've mentioned this before, but it bears repeating here. These applications are excellent tools when used correctly. They are flexible and allow a wonderful level of detail. They will accomplish everything I have talked about so far in scheduling.

They are neat, handy, clear, and extremely useful. They include Microsoft Outlook and others that are all about equal. If you use a computer at your work-place, this is the way to go.

Assignment

Look into an electronic calendar program for your computer. Find one you like and start using it to build your daily schedule.

Epilogue

These applications also come with other very useful tools besides a calendar, including an electronic To Do List and an address book. Both are extremely useful and can be linked to your calendar.

48

Make the Electronic Calendar Work

If you choose to use an electronic calendar, you need to understand how to make it work best for you in managing your time. Each is a little different, but they all have some capabilities that are the same.

First, make certain you update it every day. EVERY day. Remember that scheduling is a daily activity, but updating the calendar is an almost hourly activity. Remember that contingency time? You will need to adjust that as it happens, not as you originally scheduled it. Contingencies rarely happen as you plan them.

Second, use the tool. Refer to it constantly. I keep my calendar on my desktop as my primary screen when not working on something else.

Third, use the special functions in these programs. Most will let you have little pop-ups that come on the screen to remind you of activities. You can set the time for reminders—say, 15 minutes before or 10 minutes before. Use them; they help.

> ### *Assignment*
>
> Use the calendar. Refer to it, update it, and use its tools. Use that PDA as well, so long as you remember to synchronize it with the computer calendar.

Fourth, synchronize to your PDA routinely, if you use a PDA (which I recommend). Then you have your calendar with you all the time.

Epilogue

Electronic calendars and PDAs are extraordinarily useful in organizing your time. Don't ignore this technology. It's really useful.

49

Attend Outside Meetings

We all have to attend outside meetings. It just goes with the territory in the modern world of work. If you don't, you are lucky!

> **Assignment**
>
> Plan outside meetings carefully. Plan the time for the meeting, the time to travel, and the time to prepare.

But those outside meetings take time. Not just the meeting time itself, but also preparation time and travel time. So they can be very time-expensive.

Make the most of these meetings when you have to attend. But also make certain that they are scheduled on your calendar, that you have scheduled travel time to get to the meeting location and back, and that you have scheduled some preparation time to get ready for the meeting.

Use the time while you are traveling to the meeting for other purposes. Refer to Ideas 124–130 for some good ideas on how to use travel time efficiently.

Epilogue

Too many times I have watched friends and coworkers have to crisis manage their schedules because they forgot a meeting or forgot to plan travel time, or failed to build in time to prepare for a meeting and ended up burning the midnight oil to get ready. Don't let this happen to you.

50

Minimize Interruptions: Set Office Hours

Remember when you were in college and those professors always limited meetings with them outside class time to a small set of office hours? I do. And it always hacked me off that they limited access to themselves. It was not until after I graduated that I realized why they had to do that.

It was not that they didn't like talking to students. It was that they all had a hundred students or more every semester in their classes. If they just let them come by any old time, they would never get any other work done (preparing for classes, grading papers, and so forth). So they tried to group all that into one set of times every semester.

> **Assignment**
>
> Set office hours for internal visits and coordination. Then publish those hours so everyone knows about them.

They were controlling their time. And you need to do that as well. I do, now that I understand what they were doing. I set specific hours very day for people who work in the office to come by and see me. Those times are posted on my door. (Yep, I'm lucky. I have a door.) I also get people used to the idea. I also put these times in my schedule.

Now I control when my interruptions happen. And it's at times when I'm doing administrative or low-priority work so the interruptions are not significant.

Epilogue

This will not be foolproof. The boss won't care about your office hours. Others will ignore them or forget. But many will honor them, and you will reduce your interruptions during more productive times.

51

The Second-Greatest Time-Killer

The second-greatest time-killer is communication—that is to say, unnecessary, inefficient, time-consuming communication. We spend too much time talking with others, writing memos to each other, writing and sending e-mails to each other, leaving voice mails with each other, and so on.

And chatting on the telephone is the single greatest time-killer of them all. We are not organized in our calls so we ramble all over the topic using far too much time. Most people don't think through what they want to talk about before they pick up the phone and punch the speed dial. That leads to

Assignment

When you make phone calls to trade information, get some information, or get a decision, write down what you are to accomplish on the call first. Then follow your notes.

very inefficient telephone conversations fraught with confusion, chaos, misunderstandings, and dropped responsibilities.

If you do nothing else from these next several ideas, think before you dial. Identify exactly what information you want to convey or decision you need and jot it down in writing before making that call. Stay on task and on topic, using your notes, and you'll find that you are much more efficient at using the telephone.

Epilogue

You'll find an enormous time savings using this method. If you time your calls, you'll find you often save half the time over previous such calls. You'll also develop a reputation for efficiency by using this simple method.

52

Handle Voice Mail

Voice mail is a wonderful invention. It's a digital realm where everyone can leave a message as long or short as they wish, as detailed as they wish, and on any subject they wish.

And that's the problem. They do! You get messages about everything. For example:

"Hi, Steve, this is Frank Jones. Just wanted to check with you about our meeting tomorrow. My calendar shows 10 a.m. in the second floor conference room. Just checking." Click.

Well, that was useful. It's on you calendar, too. So what was the point? To make it worse, Frank has a cubicle four down from yours!

Assignment

Tell people to e-mail you instead of leaving voice mails. Use your DND function to buy some concentrated work time.

How many times a day to you get these time-wasting voice mails? Individually they do not take much time to listen to, but collectively over the course of a day, they can use 15–20 minutes. What to do?

A few ideas:

- ◆ Encourage people to come see you rather than leave voice mails—especially office colleagues.

- ◆ Be efficient (ruthless!) in deleting them when you hear the basic message.

- ◆ Discourage long messages—encourage e-mail instead. (More on e-mail later.)

Another tip: Most telephone systems have a "do not disturb" (DND) function that allows you to send all phone calls to voice mail. When you need concentrated time to get something done, set your phone on DND. You'll pay for that later with a number of voice mails, but it buys you an undisturbed time to get some work done.

Epilogue

The next time Frank wants to leave you a silly voice-mail message, maybe he'll just come down the hall and look in your door.

53

Your Voice-Mail Message

Recording the right voice-mail message on your system is the key to controlling what you get in return. Be encouraging, but limiting. All too often, this is what we hear:

"Hi, this is Steve. Sorry I missed your call. Leave me a detailed message, your name, and your phone number, and I'll get back to you as soon as I can."

This message is license for someone to steal time from you in massive quantities. "A detailed message?" Why? They'll take five minutes just telling you that they need to talk to you about something and give you all the gory details you already know!

You can control your incoming messages by controlling what you ask people to do in your initial message. Try something such as this:

> ### Assignment
>
> Change your outgoing voice-mail message to reflect something that resembles mine. Be encouraging, but request brief messages with just a subject.

"Hi, this is Steve. Sorry I missed your call. Briefly tell me the subject of your call, your name, and your phone number, and I'll get back to you as soon as I can."

Notice the differences?

First is the key word: *briefly*. It encourages a message, but a short one.

The second is the word *subject*. It encourages not a long story with all the gory details, but a simple idea of the topic the person wants to address. Using this message has cut my voice-mail message lengths in half! Yes, sometimes I still get people who leave a long one, but most honor what they hear. It works!

Epilogue

You'll find most of your messages will be shorter, more direct, and succinct, and you'll save another amount of time you can use for other things.

54

Use Voice Mail as a Call-Screener

When you want to get some uninterrupted work time in, use your voice mail to screen calls, especially if you don't want to use the "do not disturb" function for fear of missing something important.

Set your voice mail to go to your speaker (if you have one) and keep working when a call comes in. Listen to the caller to identify if it is someone you should break concentration for to answer, or just let him or her finish the message and call him or her back later.

Assignment

Try this method for a week. If you can become comfortable with it, keep going. If not, go back to your regular mode. Perhaps the "do not disturb" function is better for you.

This takes the ability to multitask a bit, as you keep working and listen at the same time. But even if you stop for just a minute to listen, if you choose not to take the call, you are right back to work on your project instead of involved in a long phone conversation that takes you away form work and steals more time from you.

This doesn't work for everyone. Some don't have phone systems that will support this. Others can't split their attention easily. But for those who can use this method, it's another simple time-saver that allows you to be more efficient and effective.

Epilogue

You can save as much as 10 minutes a day using this method. That may not sound as though it's very much, but 10 minutes a day, times five days a week is 50 minutes. That's almost an hour a week saved!

55

Use Caller ID Effectively

Here's a real time-saver: caller ID. If your system supports caller ID, use it. It will allow you to save lots of time not answering calls.

It's really simple. Program all the phone numbers of the people you communicate with most into your phone. Then, as calls come in, simply look to see who's calling you. If it's someone you can delay or put off until later, let the call go to voice mail. If not, take the call.

Assignment

Program your phone with all of the key people you communicate with on a regular basis. Yes, this takes some initial time, but it will allow you great control later in determining which calls you take immediately and which you let go to voice mail and listen and respond to when it's a better time for you.

Caller ID puts you in charge of your incoming calls and allows you to determine when you deal with them. Of course, it doesn't work for any call from a number not programmed into your system, but then you can make a determination about taking that call or not.

Epilogue

Although not everyone has this capability, when you do, Caller ID puts you in charge of the phone, not the phone in charge of you!

56

Handle Inbound Phone Calls

One way to control your time better is handling your incoming phone calls more efficiently.

Most of us want to be, and are, pleasant and nice people. Unfortunately, that costs us time on phone calls. Why? Because we spend too much time talking about things that are not relevant to the purpose of the call in the first place. Here's just half of a conversation:

"Hey, Steve, how are you? How's Sally? That's good. I hear you guys are planning a vacation next month. Where are you going? Yeah, been there, wonderful place. You enjoy that vacation. Yes, Fred's off to college this fall. I just don't know what it's going to be like with him gone from the house...." And so on. Then, "So, anyway, the reason I called is...."

I listen to people complain about not having enough time for their work, and then listen to their phone calls, where they all spend far too much time on this kind of chatter and too little time on the purpose of the call.

Control your natural desire to chat. Keep people who call you focused on the purpose of the call.

> **Assignment**
>
> The next time someone calls you and goes into one of these personal updates, try this: "Frank, sorry to interrupt, but let's catch up at lunch some day. I'm on a short deadline right now on a project and need to get going on it. What can I do for you?" Yes, it sounds a little abrupt, but it gets the caller back on track, and you back to work more quickly.

Epilogue

Remember that, although this buys you time, you still want those relationships, so make a point of catching up with the "chat" later over lunch.

57

Handle Outbound Phone Calls

Calls you make can suffer from the same problems: the personal chatter. Control your own personal chatter and you'll save time.

But they can also suffer from a lack of organization. Here's an example:

"Hey, Frank, how are you? Say, I need to talk about this conference coming up in March. Yeah, I think it's the 22nd and 23rd. Okay, let me make sure, hold on. (pause) Yes, 22nd and 23rd. My question is, who makes the arrangements for the meeting rooms? Oh, I don't know. Let me see if I have that information." (pause) And it goes on this way for many minutes as you have to look up information to have the conversation.

These pauses to look up information waste time. Be prepared for your calls by getting out all of your information ahead of time,

Assignment

The next time you need to make a coordination phone call, get out all your information in advance, review it, and make a couple of quick notes on what you need to accomplish during the call.

organizing it, and knowing what you want to ask and what you expect from the other party. Organization with a couple of notes will save enormous amounts of time for both of you.

Epilogue

You will be amazed at the time savings you get during these coordinating phone calls when you start them with some organization. After all, you would do that for a personal meeting—so why not a phone meeting?

58

Keep Written Records of Phone Calls

Keeping written records of your phone calls doesn't sound as if it will save any time, does it? Yet it will. How many times have you had a telephone conversation one day and then a few days later no one can remember what was decided? Or worse, there is confusion or disagreement about what was decided.

All of this confusion and disagreement will cause a great deal of time and personal angst to overcome and correct—more time than just jotting down a few notes after every phone call to record what was decided and/or what information was passed.

It really is quite simple. You will probably have a

Assignment

Keep a tablet or small notepad at hand for recording decisions and information passed during telephone conversations. Write neatly and clearly, but brevity is also important. Then file it with the project paperwork.

file or a record of each project or task you are working on. Just complete your phone call, and write down on a piece of paper, perhaps just a memo pad, what was decided and what information was exchanged. Handwritten is fine.

Then just file it. It will be there when others in the call have forgotten or remember the conversation differently. When they do, you'll have your written record of what actually occurred. You'll save time and save trouble later.

Epilogue

I can't tell you how many times having a brief memo to myself about what happened during a telephone conversation has "saved my bacon" and saved me lots of time and trouble. It will save you the same.

59

Speaking Is Faster Than Writing Memos

Frank is a fairly typical office manager. He supervises about 10 people and really knows his job. But he likes to send memos! Lots and lots of memos. In fact, Frank will send a memo to a single person that is only two sentences long!

I once asked Frank why he did that. He said that he thought it was more appropriate and formal and that it was the right way a manager should communicate with people. I suggested that he might be more effective if he had more personal conversations. I also suggested that it took him twice as much time to write memos to his employees as it did to just tell them verbally.

He suggested that I was wrong about the time (he actually said it a little more strongly than that!) and challenged me on it.

I bet him to track the time he took during one week to write memos to his employees—and then track the time it took to just verbally tell them the second week. If it turned out I was wrong and he saved no time, I would buy him dinner at the best steak place in town. He took the bet.

> **Assignment**
>
> Tell, don't write. It also increases your personal interactions with employees.

Guess what? I didn't have to buy that steak dinner! He agreed he took about half the time to inform employees verbally than it took him to write the memos.

> **Epilogue**
>
> *If you want a free steak dinner, don't bet me on what takes longer—writing or telling.*

60

Handle Your Paper Mail

The mail comes into most organizations once or twice a day. And it gets delivered to you the same way. However, all too often, we feel as if, once that mail has arrived, we have to handle it. Why? It just spent two or three days getting to us, so it can't be too timely.

Yet we almost always want to open and read the mail as soon as it arrives, even if it breaks into something else we are doing, causing disruption to our work and costing time.

Don't let the timing of the mail delivery dictate your life and work habits. When it arrives let it sit there until you have time to deal with it. Better yet, create a routine for handling the mail. You know when it comes in every day, so just establish a time every day when you open and read or process it. But it does NOT have to be when it arrives.

Assignment

Leave the mail until the end of the day when all of your tasks for the day are complete—or as complete as you can make them for that day. It's a nice way to end the day, and, if there are things that have to be taken care of in the mail, you can set aside scheduled time the next day to handle them. That way, the mail doesn't interrupt your workday.

Epilogue

Don't let the mail's arrival disrupt and dictate your schedule. Take control of it—don't let it control you.

61

Handle Your E-mail: When

E-mail is a wonderful thing. It has provided a significant tool in our communication arsenal. But it can also be a huge time-consumer!

We all tend to receive far too much e-mail. One way to control the flow of e-mail is to control when you look at it. Most e-mail applications, including Microsoft Outlook, allow you to control how often the program goes out and gets new e-mail messages. It also allows you to set an alert to pop up on your monitor screen when new messages arrive.

Control this interruption, because it will interrupt you! The message pops up over any application you are working in and will distract you. There are three things you can do:

Assignment

Adopt one or all of these suggestions. Use the Help function in your application if you don't know how to do these things.

1. Disable the message function so it does not interrupt you.
2. Set the application to check for new e-mail at a longer frequency. Instead of every 15 minutes, set it for 30 minutes, or 45 minutes, or even more.
3. Deal with e-mails in batches, not just a few at a time.

Epilogue

Although this will not save major chunks of time, reducing the distractions could easily save you five to 10 minutes a day. Combined with a few other of these ideas, you could save a significant portion of your workday.

62

Handle Your E-mail: Brevity

Many of us write e-mail messages constantly all day long. One way to save time is to understand that e-mail is an informal communication method. Long messages are not as effective as short ones. And they take more time.

Write short, direct e-mail messages. They should not read the way letters or complete memos do. If they do, you should be writing that kind of communication, not an e-mail.

Try to encourage others with whom you communicate to write succinctly as well. It is significantly more effective and far more efficient.

Assignment

Practice writing shorter e-mail messages. Make a note and post it on your monitor to remind you that "shorter is better."

Epilogue

As with most of these ideas, this one will not save massive amounts of time. But combined with others about handling e-mail, it could easily save you 30 minutes a day!

63

Handle Your E-mail: Files

I can't tell you how many times I have consulted with people and discovered that their e-mail in-box has 900 or more messages in it! They can't find anything. Even when they search or sort, it's a time-consuming process.

The best way to manage e-mail messages that you need to keep for any reason is to set up files for them. All e-mail applications allow you to do this. Determine your best filing system, perhaps by person,

Assignment

Decide what filing system (labels) will work best for you and then establish a set of files for your incoming (and perhaps sent) messages. Establish it, and then use it routinely.

or by department, or by project or…you get the drift. Create folders for them in your in-box and then, once you have read or responded to one, simply drag it into the folder and drop it there. Then, when you need to find it again, it's in the obvious folder and you'll be able to find it quickly. You can do the same for sent messages if you want.

Epilogue

It takes a little extra time to set up, but once it's established it is easy to use in this "drag and drop" world. You'll be very happy about having it the next time you have to find a message someone sent you.

64

Handle Your E-mail: Fight Spam

Spam has become the bane of our electronic existence these days. Far too much of our inbound e-mail is spam or spoof or other ways to get to us with marketing messages. For some, up to half of their messages are junk mail. But there are ways to combat this nuisance.

First, make certain your network administrator has a system for screening out known spam. Second, when you identify spam, tell your e-mail application to identify any further messages from that e-mail address as spam and automatically put it in a spam or junk e-mail folder.

Assignment

If you don't already have an anti-virus program (such as Norton or McAfee) running on your machine, add one or talk to your network administrator about adding it as soon as possible. Then always identify junk mail so your applications can screen those message out routinely.

Finally, make certain you have an anti-virus application running on your computer. Most have spam protection and elimination functions you can use to help eliminate such unwanted messages.

Epilogue

You'll spend a little time arranging all of these suggestions, but it will be worth it. You could save another five to 10 minutes a day by not having to review and delete the unwanted e-mails you receive.

65

E-mail: Discourage the Jokers

You've all seen this. The friend or colleague who constantly sends you the "joke of the day" or some great cartoons, or the latest urban legend story that usually turns out to be fiction. They are always enjoyable, but they also eat into the time available for getting things done.

There was a point I was receiving five or 10 of these a day from various friends and co-workers. And, of course, I always had to read them. Fun, but it usually ate up 15–30 minutes every day! I finally decided a little "tough love" was needed—for myself.

I simply e-mailed all my friends and asked them not to send these messages to me. I asked them to send anything appropriate to business or anything that was truly remarkable, but to stop sending them as a daily routine. As an excuse, and to make it more friendly, I told them my network administrator had asked everyone to reduce the amount of message traffic on our e-mail server.

> **Assignment**
>
> Identify everyone who routinely sends you this kind of e-mail and ask them to reduce it to only the absolutely remarkable stuff. The really good stuff.

These messages stopped. Because I was polite and passed on the blame, I lost no friends or colleagues. And I saved a bunch of time every day. And I still get the really good ones!

Epilogue

I saved at least 15 minutes every workday with this method. That's an hour and 15 minutes every week I got back from a very small investment. You will, too.

66

E-mail: Organize Your Folders

After I set up folders for my in-box and sent files in Outlook (my e-mail application), I discovered I had quite a few. Running through the list started to be time-consuming. Then I hit on the easy solution: Simply put the most used files—the ones where I receive and send most messages—at the top of the list.

That made it quick and easy to file most of my messages via "drag and drop." Of course, I occasionally need to adjust them based on which projects are most current or active, but that is a relatively simple thing to do.

Assignment

Organize your folders so that the most used are at the top of your list and the least used are at the bottom. Adjust as things change.

Epilogue

Just this small action saves me a minute every time I check my e-mail. Because I do that about 10 times at day, I figure I'm saving about 10 minutes every day just with good file organization. You'll do the same. A little here and a little there adds up!

67

E-mail: Write Clear and Direct Subject Lines

So what does writing clear subject lines have to do with saving time?

You'd be surprised how effective a well-written subject line will shorten response times to your e-mails. And the quicker you get responses, the more efficient you can be.

Assignment

Concentrate on writing active and clear subject lines to your e-mail messages. Encourage others to do so as well; you'll all save time and things that are important will move faster.

How many times do you get e-mails with the subject: Widget (or other) Project? What's in the e-mail? Does it require action? Is it just for information? Are you a primary recipient or just copied on it? You don't know from such a general subject line.

Subject lines such as "Widget Project Decision Needed," "New information on Widget Project," and "Answer to your Widget questions" are much more revealing and will get you quicker responses or actions when you need them. This helps keep your actions from being quite so fragmented.

Epilogue

The basic time-saver here is quickness of responses that allows you to be more efficient in your projects and tasks. More efficient = less time.

68

Copy and Paste Are Two of Your Best Friends

Modern computers are wonderful. They have provided us with many time-saving tools. One of the very best is also one of the most simple: copy and paste. If you already did not know this, you can copy text from one document and paste it right into another. Okay, you knew that.

Did you know that you can do that no matter what program or application you are using? You can copy data or text from a spreadsheet program and paste it right into a word processing document.

> **Assignment**
>
> Check the various programs you use for instructions (use Help) on how to copy and paste. You might even want to discover the keyboard shortcuts for copy and paste to make it even faster.

You can also copy from Websites and your e-mails right into word processing documents. Don't ever retype anything you have in electronic form anymore. Just copy and paste.

Epilogue

I love copy and paste. I don't retype anything anymore. And I have learned it saves an enormous amount of time. However, remember not to copy and use copyrighted materials from a Website without the Website owner's permission. A note of caution: always double-check your copied text for any missing punctuation you might have skipped.

69

Handle Office Visits

Frank comes into your office (okay, your cubicle!), sits down in your guest chair uninvited, and asks how you are doing. He then engages you in personal conversation about your daughter's school recital and his son's baseball game last night, repeats an office rumor about one of the VPs, and then, after five to 10 minutes of banter, finally gets to the reason for his visit: the Widget Project.

He's just killed 10 minutes of your day. How many times does this happen in a week? How much time do you lose with these encounters?

> ### Assignment
>
> Learn to stand up if you want to shorten these unscheduled office visits. If some personal time is appropriate to maintain the relationship, then okay, but do so selectively.

How do you keep this from happening? It's so simple you'll kick yourself. Just stand up.

Yep, just stand up as soon as he comes in the office. Seeing you standing, he (and most people) will not choose to sit down in your office. If he doesn't sit down, he probably will not be as comfortable and will skip the banter and get to the point. Savings: five to seven minutes every time it happens.

Epilogue

Want to improve that? Instead of letting Frank talk first, stand up and you take charge of the conversation. "Hey, Frank. How are you?" (Don't wait for an answer!) "What can I do for you?" That will get him on topic right away.

70

Handle Paper Files

All that paperwork. Where does it all come from, anyway? Is it in stacks on your desk? Piles on the floor? Organized in files in your desk? Can you easily find what you need quickly? I find that most people can't. And they lose time and efficiency finding the things they need. Computers did NOT do away with paper.

The solution: Create an organization that works for you—your solution. Here's mine, and one adopted by many:

I have three "racks" on my desk for file folders. One rack holds projects I'm working on now that are hot. One contains projects that are long-term and that I work with occasionally. The third contains reference files for office information, client information, and so forth.

Everything else is in my desk drawer or in a file cabinet in a hanging file system I organized to suit my needs (not some office manager's system!). It's pretty simple. The stuff on my desk is current and things I'm working on. Supporting information goes in the desk drawer in hanging file folders marked with the project name—nothing more. As folders on my desk get too big, I move documents to the drawer. The desk files are lean and mean!

Everything else, and I mean everything, is in the cabinet organized the same way: by project name. To aid in organization I just use an alphabetical order.

Assignment

Create your own filing system that puts your immediate needs at hand, and your less-immediate information and documents in storage.

91

Epilogue

You can keep just what you need right at hand for immediate retrieval quite easily if you are disciplined about it.

71

Magazines: Cull and Kill

You have to get them. Magazines. We all do. Keep up with the industry; keep up with the market; keep up with the community. But some—well, who knows why we get them.

A couple of years ago I did an inventory of all the magazines and professional publications I was getting. It was astounding! I was getting more than 25 different monthly publications. Did I read all of them? Of course not. So why did I constantly junk up my office with these things?

We don't have a waiting room the way physicians and dentists do, so where do they go? Do you have something similar? Here's what I did.

I went through each one carefully, including at least two issues of each publication. I made some critical choices, separating into three piles: one for those I read consistently, one for those I found I never read (the "kill" stack), and one for those I occasionally read something from. I immediately cancelled subscriptions to those I never read.

Assignment

Cull out those publications you don't need or read and "kill" them.

For the other two categories, I kept them but monitored the occasional stack. After a while, I ended up "killing" about half of those as well. That reduced my reading time significantly.

Epilogue

As I thought about this, I suggested the idea to a number of colleagues in other businesses. They all complained of the same problem and applied my solution, and it has saved them time.

72

Use a "Reading File"

Once you have decided what to keep and what to get rid of, when do you read it? When do you read all that other office information that comes in on a daily basis? If you try to consume all that information as it comes in, you end up fragmenting your day and losing time to inefficiency.

Instead, consider creating a Reading File. This is a file folder full of reading material you want to get to, but don't need to read right away: magazines, reports, administrative memos, and so forth. You decide. Let that file build up for a few days, perhaps

Assignment

Set up a Reading File for yourself and try this technique. First try every few days and then try to extend that to a week. Find out what works best for you.

a week. Then carve out some dedicated time to run through that information.

Many I've talked to over the years say the best time to do that is either early in the morning, once a week, at the end of a day (not Friday, though), or they take the file home on a weeknight or weekend.

My own preference is a nice weekend read on the patio with a cool one by my side!

Epilogue

You will save time here by concentrating this reading at one time rather that having it fragment your worktime throughout the day or week.

73

Create a Contact List

Make your computer work more effectively for you by using an application that allows you to create an electronic contact list. There are lots of them out there. If you use Microsoft Office, you probably have Outlook. It allows you not only to create a name/address/telephone list, but to add personal things such as birthdays and e-mail addresses. You can use most of them as well to record contacts with the person.

This saves time finding things because it's electronic, and it also lets you record phone calls, office visits, decisions made, and so on, so you have that information available every time you call or visit that person. This saves you having to look up all that information in notes in some misplaced file folder somewhere.

And because it's digital, you can update changes very easily and quickly without fuss or muss.

Assignment

Create a digital contact list you can keep current.

I use one that allows me almost immediate access to phone numbers of people I call. No looking anything up in some handwritten list or looking in directories. How much time do I save? Probably only a few minutes every day. Again, though, a minute here and a minute there, and you've saved a lot of time.

Epilogue

I also use it when I receive calls. When someone calls me, I immediately pull up his entry and can see the notes from our last meeting, note his wife's name, and the annotation about his son's aspiration to become a lawyer. It's a great relationship tool.

74

Use a PDA

You already know what a PDA is—a personal data assistant. But do you use one? Resisting that technology? Why? These things are great for having information right at your fingertips. They are small, easy to use, easy to keep up to date, and quite inexpensive these days.

What can it do for you?

Assignment

Get one! If you are technophobic, don't worry. They really are quite simple. Then start using it. I have used one for years and find it to be a great time-saver when I am out of the office. I can make calls when I'm out of the office quickly and easily while I'm driving (do so cautiously and safely!) and make excellent use of time that's otherwise non-productive.

It will keep your calendar for you, and synchronize it with your computer as well, which is great for times out of the office.

It will maintain your entire contact list as well (see Idea 73). Need to make a phone call while you're out of the office? No sweat. Check your PDA for Frank's phone number. It's synched from your computer, too.

Do you use a task list? I hope so! PDAs can handle those easily. And, of course, if you want the real gold standard of PDAs, get a mobile phone that is also a PDA.

Not only do PDAs save you from having to manually keep a calendar or, worse, a manual telephone listing, they are current as long as you synch with your computer.

Epilogue

This small item can save lots of time on the road and out of the office by helping you use downtime efficiently.

75

Make It Really Save Time—Not Use More Time

All these new technologies we are seeing are touted to save us time in our lives. Unfortunately, not all of them actually do that. Some require such vast amounts of set-up expertise that help is required. Others require constant maintenance. Yet others, many others, never seem to live up to their promises of saving time.

I have a colleague who is a classic "early adopter." If it's new technology, he'll buy it. He is always looking for that new "time-saving" device. Unfortunately, most of the time he is disappointed because, although they are always innovative and interesting, they rarely really save him any time. But he is undeterred and will jump at the next device as soon as it's available.

Beware of the "geeks bearing gifts" syndrome. The idea that all new technology will save time and money is simply proving wrong. Some do. When they do, adopt them. But wait until they prove themselves.

Assignment

Resist the impulse to get the newest and best. Wait until they are mainstream and have proven themselves as true time-savers before you take the leap.

Epilogue

Remember: The time you save WILL be your own. So let others discover what works and does not work.

76

Keep Software Current

One of the easiest and best ways to save time is to make sure your software is up to date. Using old software really can cost you time. If you have to convert to other file modes, are operating with an outdated operating system on your computer, or are using a version of an application two or three generations old, you are probably costing yourself time.

Assignment

Examine the software you use routinely to see if it is out of date. If you are using old applications, investigate the new versions. You will generally find they include new ways to automate routine functions that will save you time. Upgrade as necessary.

Most updates to applications do two things: they add capabilities to the software, and they add speed and ease of use. It is this last item you should be especially interested in obtaining. As users continue to tell application developers what they want, it is ease of use that is the most common. So, developers find ways to give the user what he wants. Each new version is more capable, is much easier to use, and reduces the time it takes to accomplish the more common functions.

Epilogue

Not every upgrade is valuable as a time-saver. But you cannot know until you investigate. Even if you only save a few seconds on five routine actions, if they ARE routine, you do them all the time. A few seconds multiplied by x times a day will add up.

77

Keep Your E-desktop Clean

Jack is a colleague who does much of his work on his computer. He has a very large monitor—about 21 inches! Wish I had one that large. But I am always astounded that Jack can actually find anything on his computer. His computer desktop, the electronic desktop where you can put icons for applications and routinely used files, is completely filled. Completely!

All 21 inches of his monitor are chock full of icons for files—mostly data files, not applications. Putting icons on the desktop is for convenience and quick retrieval, not for common storage. But no, Jack has to have everything he works on, has worked on, or, apparently, will ever work on, on his desktop. And he can't find a thing! I've seen him try to find a file he has just been working on for two minutes before he can locate the right icon on the desktop. What a waste of time.

Keep your desktop clean. Put application icons and any files you are working on right now on the desktop, and put any others in appropriate file folders in My Documents. Then you can find what you need quickly and easily.

Assignment

Look over your desktop. Clean off anything that junks it up and makes it difficult to find what you need. Then routinely clean it off every week.

Epilogue

Don't be like Jack. He must lose five or six minutes every day just trying to find things that are right there in front of him!

78

Establish a Clean Filing System

Keeping your computer files organized is just as important as having organized paper files. If you want to find them fast and easily, you need a system. Computer files, whether on a PC or a Mac, reside in folders. And a logical hierarchy of folders will make all the difference in ease and quickness of use.

The easiest way to do this is to create project folders. These are the main folders for major projects, tasks, clients, customers, and so on. Into each of these you create individual folders for activities for that project. For example: I have a project folder for this book as I write it. I labeled it with the book name. Then I created a folder for business activities with my publisher and agent, one for sections in the book, and one for research. Inside each of those I have folders or files that fit those categories. In the research folder I have sub-folders for various actions I have recorded or discovered and used for this book. In the sections folder, I organize the ideas into nine different folders representing themes of the book. And so on.

> ### **Assignment**
>
> Examine your current filing system—or lack of one. Reorganize your files in a logical way so you can find things quickly and easily. Maintain that system and you'll save time finding and opening your computer files.

You should do something similar for your files to make them easy to find and use.

> **Epilogue**
>
> *You can easily save five or six minutes a day with a good, logical filing system. That's 25 minutes a week—more than three hours in a month.*

79

Make Certain Your Computer Is Operating at Speed

Computers are supposed to be fast, not slow and clunky. If you have an old computer that runs slow, then it's time for a new—and faster—computer. Today's computers, even the inexpensive ones, are very fast. But we can junk them up and slow them down. They then cost us time, not save us time.

The best way to make certain your computer is running as efficiently as possible is to routinely run (on PCs) a "scandisk" function and a "defragmentation" function. Scandisk will clean up old files such as temporary files, and defrag will reorganize your hard disk drive for optimum access to your most commonly used applications and files. If you can't figure out how to run these applications (part of Windows), use the Help function.

> **Assignment**
>
> Create a monthly schedule to run scandisk and defrag. These take a while to run, so you may want to do this over a weekend or overnight.

Macintosh computer users should use the Disk Utility in the MAC OS and follow the links to First Aid and Repair Disk. Most Mac users also use an application called DiskWarrior to manage the efficiency of their computers.

Create a monthly schedule to run "scandisk" and "defrag." These take a while to run, so you may want to do this over a weekend or overnight.

> **Epilogue**
>
> *After some months, hard drives become disorganized. Just running defrag will improve the access time for your files and applications significantly.*

80

Make Certain Your Internet Connection Is at Speed

We all operate on the Internet these days. Some could not imagine being without it! Yet it is less than 15 years old. But it has become so important a communication mechanism that we really must get the most out of it today.

Internet connection speeds are extremely important—not just for e-mail and attachments, but for visiting Websites for business purposes. Websites today are designed with the assumption of reasonable access speeds. The old dial-up speeds of 56K are simply insufficient today.

Assignment

Explore the best option for a broadband connection from two primary choices: DSL and cable. If you already have cable, that is the fastest and easiest. If not, your telephone company can probably deliver a DSL connection (slightly slower) at a reasonable cost.

Make sure you're not sitting watching your monitor as Websites slowly load or e-mails with attachments to download. A high-speed (called broadband) connection is a must today. Take advantage of the serious reduction in cost for these connections and save time as your downloads flash onto the screen in almost no time.

Epilogue

You can lose a lot of time waiting for things to happen on the Internet using a low-bandwidth (slow speed) connection. Save time with broadband.

81

Virus Protection: Not an Option

There are plenty of insidious and nasty people out there waiting to corrupt your computer. Allowing a virus or worm into your computer today can easily put you out of business for days. Talk about lost time!

So install an antivirus program immediately. There are two primary sources: Norton Antivirus and McAfee Antivirus.

Assignment

If you have an antivirus program running, good. Make certain that your subscription is up to date. If not, get a new one fast.

103

They both are reasonably inexpensive for an annual subscription and will download the latest virus definitions so your computer remains constantly protected from worms and viruses. You can find them both on the Internet and can even download them using e-commerce systems.

Epilogue

It's not a matter of if *your computer will be attacked by a virus, but* when. *Operating a computer on the Internet without antivirus protection can be likened to driving a car without wearing a seatbelt.*

82

More on PDAs

PDAs, or personal data assistants, are becoming almost indispensable in the business world today. These little numbers are highly portable and allow you to keep that task list you have already developed, your address book, and your calendar in one very portable package.

They have become quite inexpensive at the low end, and extremely expensive at the high end, where one can integrate the PDA with cellular telephone and Internet access. Take your pick, but even the inexpensive ones (I use the cheapest available and it is invaluable) allow you great flexibility to

Assignment

Look into PDAs. Research them, price them, and adopt one. Keep it synched with your computer on a routine basis (key point here) and take it with you when you travel, even around town.

do things while out of the office. During that downtime when you are waiting for things to happen—on the road, waiting for the car to be serviced, and so on—you can be doing things.

Probably the most useful item is the address book. I have my complete address book from my computer with me at all times so I can look up addresses on the road, and make phone calls by looking up phone numbers.

Epilogue

These things help you use time out of the office that otherwise would be lost to inefficiency.

83

That Cell Phone!

Okay, you gotta have one. Yes, you do. But does it rule your life? Cell phones are cheap (now) and extremely handy. They allow you to do things out of the office and make it easy for people to contact you.

So watch what you do with them. Use them, certainly. Make calls while out of the office or on the way to another location. Confirm orders, coordinate actions, set appointments, and so on. Cell phones allow

Assignment

If you don't have one, get one. If it's for business purposes, it can be used as a business expense with your taxes. Make use of it to allow greater productivity during times out of the office. Get more from the time you have available using a cell phone.

you to maximize your time away from the office in ways we could not do before.

But also don't let the darn thing rule your life, either! Don't take a call just because the phone rings. All phone services come with voice mail today, so let that call go to voice mail rather that allow it to interrupt a meeting or conversation, or ruin your concentration.

Epilogue

Although a cell phone will save you time and make you more efficient and reachable, it can also take over your life. Don't let it.

84

Who Knows Your Cell Phone Number?

Do you give your cell phone number to everyone? If so, you are giving them license to steal time from you. They'll call you at all hours, at the most inconvenient times, when you can least afford the time to take their calls.

Assignment

Review your contacts who have your cell phone number. Start limiting who you give that number to so you control who calls you, not the other way around.

A very good business practice is to limit the people to whom you give your cell phone number to those who are most important. Don't let just anybody call you. Control who has access to you via your cell phone. That way, when the phone rings, you know it's someone important to you, not your local hardware store telling you an order has arrived.

Don't put your cell phone number on business cards or other materials that everyone has access to. Make having your cell phone number a privilege, not a right. Keep that number for people you want to hear from.

Epilogue

You can waste a lot of time on phone calls from people you really did not need to hear from at times when you needed to concentrate on other tasks. You take control of that phone, don't give up control to others.

85

Cell Phone: Set to Stun

Star Trek brought us "Beam me up, Scotty" and "Set your phasers to stun." It was a fun TV show with some interesting lessons. Of course, we all experience times when we just wish Scotty could beam us up and away from a difficult situation.

But one of the best ways to control your time is to control when you answer your cell phone. If you have

Assignment

Set your cell phone to vibrate or "stun." As a general rule, keep it there unless you are in a situation were a ring tone is needed. If you are busy, let inbound calls go to your voice mail and ignore the vibration. Stay concentrated on the task at hand.

107

it set to a loud ring tone or music, it goes off and interrupts what you are doing, and maybe others as well. The easy answer is to set it to "stun" or vibrate. Phones that vibrate only boether the recipient, and they are much easier to ignore than a ring tone.

This way, you can choose to answer ot not answer depending on your current situation. If you are in the middle of an important meeting, you can ignore it. If you will be concentrating on an important task, ignore it. If you are in the waiting room for a physician's appointment, answer it. When you ignore it, it goes to your voice mail and you can check that later—at a time much more convenient to you.

Epilogue

Cell phones are wonderful and I'm a big fan. But I want to be in charge of when I answer, not leaving that to my callers. You can disrupt your day easily by answering every call that comes in as it comes in, and disruption costs time.

86

To BlueTooth or Not to BlueTooth

So what is BlueTooth? It's a wireless protocol that allows electronic equipment to communicate with each other. You see it every day with those people walking around with earpieces in one ear and who seem to be talking to themselves. They are using a BlueTooth-enabled earpiece to link to their cell phone and can make or answer calls without their phone (it's on their belt) and hands-free.

BlueTooth-enabled cell phones are wonderful, and allow you to communicate clearly and efficiently with both hands free to drive, use your computer, take notes, and so forth. If you do a lot of this kind of work, then a BlueTooth-enabled phone is for you. It can save you time by allowing you more freedom to do other things while talking on the phone.

Assignment

If you do a lot of cell phone work, look into a BlueTooth-enabled phone. It may well save you time by allowing more freedom in your calls. And many new cars are now BlueTooth-enabled as well, so you can run the phone through your car's audio system hands-free (and thus safer).

Epilogue

Just remember that, although these devices are time-saving and handy, you need to be conscious of others around you in your conversations.

87

Is Text Messaging for You?

Instant text messaging is the communications tool of teenagers today. They are on it all the time. But it can have excellent business applications as well. I use instant messaging with business colleagues when I'm at my desk for extended periods. It runs in the background and I only get a notice when someone on my buddy list sends me a message. We can have a quick and efficient conversation electronically right there at the computer. And while he's answering, I'm working.

This is a very efficient and time-saving communication tool. Windows offers this via Windows Messenger. AOL offers one, and others do, too. Unfortunately, most are unique to

Assignment

Examine instant messaging to see if you can get some efficiencies out of it. Try one or two different systems and find out which is best for you. Discuss with working partners to ensure they would use it.

their system, but most are also free. Both parties (or more if you want) need to be using the same system. Some also offer video messaging.

But if you are not technically minded or not good at multitasking, this communication tool will take more time than it saves. You decide.

Epilogue

We use this routinely both in my office as well as with business partners out of the office. It is really a time-saver for simple coordination and information-sharing tasks.

88

Get Your Own Printer!

Many of you are in cubicles or offices without a printer to print your written work. I have been in that situation many times. At first, I thought, this makes sense. Why have hundreds of printers when we can all share one large one down the hall?

Then I did a study of how much time I used walking back and forth to the printer to get printed materials. I examined this over a week's time and discovered that I spent more than half an hour just walking down the hall and back. This did not include the impromptu conversations that occurred each time!

> **Assignment**
>
> Do your own analysis. If you, too, find this kind of result, use the data to talk your boss into an inexpensive laser printer.

Then I looked into the cost of laser printers. To my surprise, I discovered that an inexpensive laser printer can be had for less than $100! For the cost of a $100 printer (yes, I ran out immediately and bought one) I can save two hours of productive work time every month.

> **Epilogue**
>
> *Not only does this save real time, but it also keeps the fragmentation of the day down so I can continue to concentrate on jobs, not wandering the halls. It's a no-brainer!*

89

Get Computer Training to Get More Efficient

If you really want to get the most out of that computer application, you have to learn more about it. Many of us are self-taught, and when we teach ourselves, we really learn only the basics. One computer trainer I talked with told me that most people know how to use less than 25 percent of the capabilities of any software they use!

111

Many applications have many time-saving and work-saving functions. But most of us don't know they exist, much less how to use them. We can save time by gaining knowledge. The question is whether to learn it ourselves or attend some training.

My vote is to get some training. Armed with some knowledge about a software, we can be functional—but not expert. Yet if this software is important to us, we should know everything about it. Becoming expert will lead us to greater capabilities and more efficiencies and, yes, time savings.

Assignment

Identify the one or two programs you use the most in your work. Assess your ability with those programs and then attend some training programs designed to enhance your abilities with them.

Epilogue

You will save time in the long run. You'll be more efficient and more capable. You may learn enough to do something no one else in the office can do. It might lead to that next promotion.

90

The Third-Greatest Time-Killer

The third-greatest time-killer is meetings. That's why we all hate them so much. You've been to meetings that could have lasted 15 minutes but went an hour because of disorganization, people showing up late, lack of a coherent agenda, and many other reasons.

So we avoid them, but can't get away from them. Meetings are absolutely necessary in almost every business or organization of which I am aware. So do we avoid them or try to make them efficient? Because they are needed, let's vow to make them more efficient and waste as little time as possible.

Assignment

Vow now to be part of the solution, not part of the problem, when it comes to wasted time in meetings.

Epilogue

A recent research project conducted by the University of Iowa determined that as much as 50 percent of the time spent in meetings is wasted. We MUST fix this.

91

They Can't Be Avoided— But They CAN Be Efficient!

The basic problem with meetings is that they are horribly inefficient. That's why they waste so much time. And there are a number of things we can do to make them more efficient.

What does efficiency take? First it takes appropriate scheduling, using agendas, advanced planning by all parties, and good personal and small group communication skills. You can help your organization gain efficiency during meetings by properly preparing yourself and demonstrating that preparation at all the meetings you attend.

If no agenda has been provided, ask for one.

> ### Assignment
>
> Set a goal to become a better meeting participant— and more active participant. Use the ideas that follow to improve your meeting skills.

If the time is not limited by the agenda, ask for that at the beginning of the meeting.

Read some materials on how effective meetings should be conducted.

Lead your work team to more efficient meetings by modeling good meeting preparation and behavior. Communicate your preparation to others and they will begin to follow your lead. And your meetings will gradually become more efficient and waste less and less time.

Epilogue

The only way to begin to eat away at that 50 percent efficiency rate at meetings is to start with yourself. Others will follow.

92

Meeting Timing—When Is Best?

Selecting the right time for meetings is the first step in more efficient meetings. If meetings take place during the busiest time of the workday, we should not be surprised when people don't show up, show up late, or show up unprepared. They have been focused on other tasks.

What time is the best time for meetings? Well, that often depends on the organization, but there are some general rules.

It is generally accepted that the beginning of the day is a good time for meetings. Although this is counter-intuitive, there are some excellent reasons. First, the day has only just begun and people are not yet involved in their daily routines or problems. Second, people are fresh in the morning, more alert, and better able to absorb new information or make decisions. Third, this timing allows for proper

Assignment

If you schedule meetings, make them for early morning. If you don't, try to influence those who do to better, more efficient times of the day.

preparation for the meeting, either the evening before or that morning just prior to the meeting.

Another good time is right after lunch. It is not as good as early morning, but after lunch people generally are refreshed from their work break and ready for new tasks.

The worst time, according to most experts, is at the end of the day. People are tired, trying to close out their work for the day, and reluctant to get involved with something that might take them over their departure time. They are most likely to remain detached and uninvolved in late-day or end-of-day meetings.

Epilogue

Simply changing the time of meetings has been demonstrated to improve meeting efficiency and the quality of group outputs.

93

Put a Time Limit on Meetings

Meetings should not be allowed to continue indefinitely. Meetings without time limits are license to steal time from the participants because they breed inefficiency. Unfortunately, most meetings don't have a time limit attached for the

Assignment

Assign time limits to meetings you set, and suggest time limits to meetings you attend.

group to get its work done, so they tend to be inefficient and waste time.

Every meeting should have a time limit. What that limit is depends on how much work the group has to do and how long it could be reasonably expected to accomplish that work efficiently. Either the meeting organizer or the group itself should always set a time limit for a meeting.

If you attend meetings that do not have a time limit, suggest that the group set one as the meeting starts. Or, suggest that to the organizer in advance. If you organize meetings, try to accurately assess how much time should reasonably be taken to accomplish the tasks for the meeting and set a limit to allow the group to work to a deadline. People are quite a bit more efficient when working against an established deadline.

Epilogue

In meetings I have organized over the years, I have found that setting a time limit produces high productivity and efficiency, and allows the group to get work done in a reasonable time without wasting that time. Those meetings also take less time than others I have attended without time limits.

94

Have an Agenda for Meetings

The greatest enemy of any meeting is the lack of an agenda. Of course, an agenda is simply a list of the topics or tasks the group is to accomplish during the meeting created in some logical order. Everyone has a copy and can focus on those specific tasks.

One of the distinct advantages of an agenda is that it keeps all participants on task and reduces time wasted from talking about things that are not on the agenda. One of the great time-wasters in meetings is side discussions/conversations about things the group did not meet about. It usually involves only a few people, and the remainder of the group is simply wasting their time. Agendas keep everyone on the topic(s) of the meeting.

Assignment

Use or encourage the use of agendas for every meeting.

Insist on agendas for your meetings. Explain the strengths of an agenda to the meeting leader or facilitator. If you set up meetings, make certain you create an agenda and distribute it in advance. Allow others to have input to the agenda in advance, but at the meeting stick to it.

Epilogue

A University of Iowa study, amongst others, demonstrated that using an agenda has been shown to decrease meeting time by as much as 25 percent.

95

Use the Agenda—Time the Elements

One of the more advanced techniques for using an agenda is to set time limits on the various elements of the agenda. Each action should have a fixed amount of time assigned to deal with that item.

This keeps everyone focused and on task. And, it also keeps the group from using up its allotted time without coming to the end of the agenda and having action items that do not get discussed or addressed. This problem leads to much-delayed action or groups going over their meeting

Assignment

Made sure that time limits are established for every item on the agenda. If you make the agenda, you do it. If someone else makes up the agenda, suggest it to him or her.

time to get everything done. Neither is a positive outcome.

Whoever develops the agenda should identify a time limit for each item. The person running the meeting then has a responsibility to keep discussion on track and on time.

Epilogue

The worst outcome of a meeting is when no decision is made on some items. Usually people are counting on those decisions. Assigning time limits on agenda items makes meetings efficient, limits wasted time, and gets all the work done.

96

Distribute the Agenda in Advance

This may sound as though I'm preaching to a choir that has the agenda message, but an agenda not delivered to participants in advance can be thought of the same way as giving students a test before the teacher covers the material. If participants have

Assignment

Make sure all your meetings have an agenda that is distributed at least two days prior to the meeting. When you don't organize the meeting, ask for an agenda in advance. Prompt the meeting owner to get something out early.

the agenda at least a couple of days in advance, they can prepare for issues or information items on the agenda. This allows for the maximization of time usage and efficiency.

In addition, it also allows for much more productive and useful meetings. If you've been to meetings where the agenda was distributed for the first time at the beginning of the meeting, then you know how unproductive and long those meetings can go.

Epilogue

Again, the University of Iowa study strongly suggests that distributing the agendas for meetings two days in advance can cut meeting times by as much as 25 percent.

97

Train Yourself on Conducting Meetings

Are you called upon to lead meetings on a regular basis? If so, know that leading small groups is a learned skill, not something you just happen to be able to do because you can breathe air. And most university programs don't provide you with these skills.

If you lead small groups and group meetings, get some training on how to do so efficiently. There are lots of sources.

Contact your HR office, your training office, or even your supervisor. If you run the show, look into programs conducted by the local chamber of commerce, local executive training programs by management training companies, or even get some coaching from a retired executive.

Don't try to do these without the right skills. A little training on small group dynamics goes a long way towards greater efficiency— and better outcomes.

> ### Assignment
>
> Research how you can get some additional training or education on leading small group meetings. Then take advantage of that training to increase your skill set.

> ### Epilogue
> *Remember: You weren't born with these skills, and you probably did not get them in school. They are learned skills, so get some learnin', as my country cousin would say.*

98

Train Participants and Staff on Efficient Meetings

Okay, you've got some training, but your group members also need training. No one has provided them with an education on how to participate in efficient and effective small group meetings, either.

So either get some coaching for your meeting group, or get trained yourself and provide that to your group. The more they know about how to effectively participate in a small group meeting, the better those meetings will go, the faster they will go, and the better the group outcomes will be.

Assignment

Look into finding a coach or training opportunity, even a brief one, to allow your meeting groups or teams to learn how to better participate in small group meetings.

Epilogue

Don't be afraid to invest some time in saving some time. Get some coaching or training for your team.

99

Attend Only the Meetings You Must

If you are like me, you get invited to a lot of meetings. I'm on a lot of organizational committees and get invited to at least three group meetings a week. Ouch. That's a lot of time away from my primary tasks!

I combat this time loss by reviewing the agendas in advance and determining if I really need to be at that meeting. Sometimes I discover that the group will be addressing topics I can't help them with. Sometimes they are not decision-making meetings, but just information-sharing meetings where I know there will be a written record of the meeting later.

In these cases, I sometimes choose not to attend. I'm courteous to the meeting organizer and let him or her know. I also share with him or her any insights if I have any regarding any topics under discussion, but I save my time and stay on task.

Don't be afraid to make some critical judgments about which meetings you attend. As you probably already know, not all meetings are needed or productive. You want to be there for the meaningful ones, but not use up your time on the others.

> ### Assignment
>
> Be judgmental about each meeting. Make a knowing decision about attendance. Sometimes it's based on your workload, sometimes on the topic or other items. But make critical time-saving decisions about what meetings you attend.

Epilogue

That hour-and-a-half you spend in a useless meeting might just be the time you come up with the next Big Idea.

100

The Greatest Time-Killer

The single greatest killer of your time is other people stealing it!

That's right. There are just too many opportunities for other people to take time away from your day. Visitors, phone calls, meetings, e-mails, office calls—the myriad opportunities during any working day that people have to interact with you are all potential time-wasters.

Not all, of course, but all too many interactions are unproductive and waste your time. People steal your time from you. And often, you don't even realize it. When you do, you don't know what you can do about it. You seem powerless to control this loss of time.

But you can. You have to control your work environment and time. Don't let others steal time from you. The simplest way to do that is to control access to you.

> ### Assignment
>
> Decide to control access to your time by taking charge of the human interaction opportunities others have with you. Once you do, all the following ideas will work for you.

> ### Epilogue
> *Take charge of your time and reduce or eliminate the number-one killer of your time. You could save hours a week!*

101

Communicate Your Work Style

Each of us has a particular style of work, a way that we find most comfortable and most effective for ourselves. Some like to concentrate the first couple of hours each day without interruption; others like to control the late afternoon for concentrated productive work; yet others are quite comfortable with interruptions throughout the day.

The key is to decide what your best, most productive work schedule is, and then communicate that to others. A model might be professors in college. Remember that they set firm office hours they are available each week to meet with students. At other times they were simply not available—doing research, grading papers, writing papers, and so on.

> ### *Assignment*
>
> Determine your best work schedule on a daily basis. Work in any meetings you must attend, and then communicate that to others. Sometimes the best way is to simply post a daily schedule outside your office.

Decide your best system for productivity and then post an office schedule outside your door or cubicle. Use that communication to help you control access to you, and thus your own productivity and time.

> ### Epilogue
> *You would be amazed at the time you can save by simply taking charge of your time.*

102

Adjust to Your Boss

Let's face it: the boss is in charge. He or she runs the show. So it is counterproductive to try to mold the boss to your work style or schedule. The most efficient way to work with your boss is to adjust to him or her.

125

Find out how he or she likes to interact with people and adjust accordingly. I have had many bosses over the years, with many different styles. I simply adjusted my style to theirs. Some want no interaction outside meetings. Fine. That gave

Assignment

Discover the boss's work style and adjust yours to it. You'll find once you do so, you will be more productive and actually save time.

me great freedom to control my schedule. Some wanted to drop into my cubicle at any time with information or instructions or questions. No problem. And there has been a wide variety in between.

I always accommodated the boss's style. It's easier and more efficient to adjust to the boss than to fight a fight you will lose. If the boss likes information by memo, I write memos. If she likes information in meetings only, fine, I wait until we have a scheduled meeting. If he just wants everything communicated by walking into his office and telling him, fine—I do that.

Epilogue

If you try to fit the boss into your work style, you will just be less productive, waste time, and—in the end—lose. The boss is the boss. Adjust.

103

Find a Mentor or Coach

Most of us move through life learning as we go. And we often learn the most from key people in our lives, both personally and professionally. My good friend Jerry Wilson, author of the first two books in this series, once told me that he learned most of what made him successful in life from one particular man he worked with on a regular basis for a number of years. Howard was his mentor.

One of the best things you can do to help organize yourself in the office is to find a mentor (or coach, if you wish to use that word). Look for someone who knows the business, knows how to operate successfully, and is willing to work with you to help you be more productive, efficient, and effective. And use your time better.

Assignment

Find your own mentor. Take your time and find the right person, and then meet with him or her routinely to talk about problems, challenges, and so forth. He or she can often show you ways to use your time more efficiently.

Find someone who is well respected, who you like and can work with well, and who is clearly successful. This person does not necessarily need to work in your organization, but should be someone you have ready access to and can have a continuing relationship with. Then let him or her share the tools of success he or she has learned over the years.

> **Epilogue**
> *Yes, wisdom often comes with age and experience. Borrow from that.*

104

Control Interactions With Others

It's in the little daily interactions with others that your time leaks away. Someone stops by the office to chat—five minutes lost; a colleague comes in unexpectedly to discuss a project problem—10 minutes lost; a subordinate drops by the office to ask you for some guidance on a problem he is working on—10 minutes lost; a friend from another department sticks his head in the door and asks about golf this Saturday—five minutes lost; and so on.

Individually, these interruptions don't seem too costly. But collectively, they can really add up to a major portion of your day. Just the few I mention in the previous paragraph added up to 30 minutes. If it was just 30 minutes a day, that's 2.5 hours a week you lose to others.

> **Assignment**
>
> Control people's access to you and you will control the loss of time that seems to leak away during the day to others.

You need to control access to yourself to prevent some of this. Some access is necessary, but some is not. For your subordinates, set standard office hours when you can be reached. For others, consider closing your door for long stretches to allow you to protect your time (if you have a door!). Sometimes just the organization of your office or cubicle can help.

Epilogue

Don't be rude, don't be unaccommodating, but do be protective of your time. After all, it is YOUR time.

105

The Geography of the Office

Believe it or not, how you organize your office can help you control access and control your time. Even if you have a cubicle and not a traditional office, how you arrange and use your workspace can help. Here are some tips:

Assignment

Take a look at how you have your office arranged. Using the tips here, make the changes you can to reduce "drop-ins."

- ◆ Face your primary workspace away from the door. That way, people coming by are not tempted to just "drop in."

- ◆ When you want some concentrated time, close your door (if you have one) to discourage drop-ins.

- Don't have a guest chair. With no chair guests aren't tempted to sit and take up more time even when they do come by.

- Post office hours outside your office or cubicle.

- Place a desk between you and the door, as a barrier.

- Leave your door half open—or half closed.

- Never face towards the door or opening to your cube. It encourages people.

Epilogue

Just some simple changes to the geography of your office can make a big difference in time saved by protecting you from those folks who just have to "drop by for a chat."

106

Desk Placement

Desks, and sometimes the modular furniture in cubicles, can be used as barriers to casual conversation—and wasted time. I learned early on how to use my desk as a barrier. When I have been in situations where I actually had a desk, I always placed it between the door and me. It was a barrier to visitors.

In cubicles, I tried to arrange my workspace so that my back was to the entry. That way someone who wanted to interrupt me had to do something more than just stop by. He or she had to knock or otherwise get my attention.

If you look busy, people are less likely to interrupt you. With your back to the entry, and looking busy, you will discourage casual visitors.

Assignment

Try to arrange your desk and workspace for maximum protection. Move the desk or rearrange your cubicle workspaces to put your primary work area in such a way so that your back is to the entry or door.

Epilogue

Think of your office or cubicle as your battleground. Any military person will tell you that you want to arrange the battleground to your advantage.

107

Chair Placement

There are usually two or more chairs in workspaces. I have always had the desire to have my chair and one for guests or visitors. I have found that both are potential weapons in protecting my time.

I always make certain that my chair faces me away from the entry or door to the workspace. That way people have to physically interrupt me to get my attention.

> **Assignment**
>
> Analyze your chair placement and types of chairs. Organize them to your best advantage by keeping your back to the door and having a hard-to-access guest chair that is uncomfortable.

My guest chair used to be an invitation to steal my time. It was out in the open and inviting. Now, I put that chair in an uninviting place. I have two guest chairs in my current office, but both are pushed right up against my desk and require that a visitor physically pull one out to sit in one. People tend not to do that uninvited. Thus, I can control who stays by my personal invitation—or lack of one—to sit down.

In addition, I usually make sure it's an uncomfortable chair that people may sit in once, but are reluctant to the second time. I may lose the first battle, but I usually win the war!

> **Epilogue**
> *None of this is being rude; it's controlling your time. If someone comes in who really needs to talk with you, you simply invite him or her to pull up a chair and chat.*

108

Relationships to Windows

If you are fortunate to have a window in your office or cubicle, good for you. But a window can both cause problems and be an asset. First, the problem.

Windows can be a distracter. Trapped inside on a beautiful spring day so evident outside your window, it's easy to look and daydream, thinking about the coming weekend or what you'll BBQ tonight on the grill. You've just killed five minutes!

Instead, face your primary workspace adjacent to the window. It's still there for good, natural light, but is not so easily distracting.

Now the asset. If you want to discourage visitors from sticking around, put yourself in front of a bright window with no shades. With the window behind you, you will be difficult to

> **Assignment**
>
> If you have a window, congratulations. Use it to your advantage, not disadvantage.

see in the office or cubicle and the light will be uncomfortable for the visitor. Visitors tend to stay shorter periods when they have to squint to see you.

> **Epilogue**
> *If you don't have a window, sorry about that.*

109

Discourage "War Stories"

I have a colleague who tells wonderful "war stories." You know the kind. They usually start with, "I remember when…" or "That reminds me of a time…." His stories are very interesting, and he does a great job of telling them.

Assignment

Divert or deflect those who want to drop in with their "war stories." Catch them early and you'll save a lot of time each week.

Unfortunately, his shortest story tends to be at least 10 minutes, and long stories can go for 20, easily!

So although I love hearing his war stories, I have to discourage him. A couple of war stories every day and I'm out as much as 30 minutes a day! I can't afford that kind of time loss. So, what do I do? I discourage them as soon as he starts.

I simply interrupt him as the story begins and tell him, not unkindly, that I am on a deadline to get a project or paper done and really need to get on that. I then divert him with a question about that project.

Epilogue

Remember not to be rude or impolite, and also make a mental note to revisit the story with that person. I usually try to remember to ask about that story at lunch or late in the day when I am not quite as busy. It maintains good relations with my colleague.

110

Stand and Be Counted

A few years ago I learned from a consultant a sure-fire method to reduce office visits to a minimum amount of time. When people come into your office to have a conversation with you, stand up immediately.

And stay standing the entire time without inviting them to sit. What the consultant had discovered, and I can now validate, is that people don't generally stick around if you are standing and don't sit down. If you sit down, they perceive that as an invitation to chat and they stay longer. They'll even begin to look around for a chair.

Assignment

Learn to stand and be counted (counting the minutes every day you will save). When visitors come in unexpectedly, stand and make them stand. They will be much more efficient with your time.

So don't let them do that to you if you want to minimize their impact on your time. When they come in, stand. Remain standing and don't invite them to sit. You'll find they will get right to the point and leave expeditiously.

It works! Great time-saver.

Epilogue
If this sounds rude, sometimes it feels that way. But you don't have to make it rude or unpleasant. Just stand and don't invite them to sit unless you want to spend time with them.

135

111

Learn to Say No

I have a friend who is now in the 12-step "just say no" program. Actually, it's easier than that, yet harder. She, as do all too many of us, has trouble saying the word *no*. So what happens? She ends up being the "go-to gal." Everyone knows she will always say yes, and she does.

The result? She's overworked and tired all the time, and says she always seems to get work done right at the last moment of deadline.

I took her through an analysis of her tasks one day and we discovered she was doing enough work to fill a 60-hour week! And much of it had nothing to do with her job. So we began a rehab program. She is required to say no at least once each day.

She now evaluates all these requests for help and work to make certain they fit with her personal and professional goals. She's beginning to learn to say no to those that do not fit. As a result, she recently told me her workload has decreased to about a 50-hours-a-week load. I told her to keep working at it.

Assignment

Learn to say no. Say no to the tasks that are really not yours to accomplish. Say no to those extra tasks people ask you to take on. Say no to doing someone else's work. Be strategic, but learn to say no.

Epilogue

Saying no is not limited to the workplace. All those extra things people ask for, such as coaching the soccer team or serving on a committee at your homeowners association, should also be closely evaluated so that they match your personal goals. Say no when they don't.

112

Learn to Delegate: Discover What Your Staff Can Handle

If you are a leader or manager, you will need to learn something that all managers must—or be condemned to a life of unnecessary toil: you must learn to delegate.

Few schools teach anyone how to do this, but it is a critical skill for managers and supervisors.

Delegating tasks and work is the purview of supervisors and managers—that's why they have those titles. But all too often, I have seen them incapable of doing that, and the result is managers working far too many hours and their employees having little to do.

Assignment

Learn which jobs are yours to do and which your staff can handle better and more efficiently. Then assign those jobs to your staff and supervise them; don't do the work yourself.

If you are in this situation, learn to discern what you need to do personally, and what you should be assigning to people who work for you—your staff. This requires an accurate assessment of your people and their capabilities. Many will thank you for giving them work and tasks. Those are the ones you will value the most.

Epilogue

As a young manager, one of the most difficult things for me to learn was to delegate work to others. But once I grasped that task, my life became much more in line with my expectations.

113

Learn to Delegate: Learn What Others Can Handle Better

As a supervisor, if you are one, one of your primary responsibilities is to manage your people. In doing so, you have to know what each of them is best at doing and where their weaknesses are. So, when work comes in, you must be

Assignment

Conduct a proper assessment of your team members to determine who is best at what. Then boldly assign tasks and work accordingly.

in a position to delegate that work to someone on your team BEST suited to get that work done, and done well.

This requires a real awareness of the strengths and weaknesses of your team, and then a willingness to delegate work assignments to them.

Don't get into the old position of, "If I want the job done right, I have to do it myself." I have seen more overworked managers with that philosophy, and they tend to burn themselves out quickly.

Rely on the strengths of the members of your team and you'll save yourself time in the long run.

Epilogue

Don't find yourself in the "do it myself" mode. You'll kill yourself doing it, and it will cost an enormous amount of personal time.

114

Learn to Delegate: Train Your Staff to Handle

Of course, once you've done your assessment of your team members, you will find weaknesses. Don't just assume that if one member is weak at task A, that you should never assign that kind of work to him or her. If you do, you will find yourself doing the work yourself occasionally because the others on your team are fully engaged in work and can't take on another task. Then you end up with it and the under-trained employee goes home on time while you put in yet more overtime.

Instead, once you are aware of weaknesses, work to overcome those in your team members. When a task comes in and has a reasonable time deadline, assign it to someone on your team who has not done that work before. Have him or her work with you or someone else to learn how to accomplish that work under supervision. Train him or her. It may take a little extra time for you to do so the first time, but it will pay off in time later as that employee learns how to accomplish that task.

> ### Assignment
>
> Assess your team, identify weaknesses, and then train your team members on weaknesses so you can assign tasks to them in the future.

Epilogue

Think of this as an investment. It takes an investment of your time initially, but it pays off in time back to you later as they learn how to do the work.

115

Recognize That Procrastination Is a Habit—Work to Break It

There are those who procrastinate and those who do not. If you are not a procrastinator, don't read this section; it's not for you.

But if you are, then here are some ideas that will help you.

First, decide if you procrastinate. As with any other addiction, the first step is to admit you have a problem. Quite frankly, you all know who you are. It's something we know in ourselves. So, if you are a procrastinator, you continually put off work until the last minute possible. This costs you added stress, pressure, and time working late to get done what should have been done much earlier.

So the first step is to admit it to yourself by looking for those signs of putting things off until it's almost too late. Then decide you are going to do something about it. You are going to put the brakes on this habit, this tendency to put things off.

Some of the ideas already presented in this book will help you both to recognize your habit and to overcome it. The following ideas are some special thoughts on procrastination and the time it costs us.

Assignment

Realize that if you are a procrastinator, it's costing you a lot of time and that the sooner you recognize that the sooner you can begin to deal with the problem.

Epilogue

Some studies of procrastination have shown that those tasks that are delayed by procrastination can cost up to twice as much time to accomplish as those that are not.

141

116

Don't Put It Off, Wimpy!

Now that you realize that you have this problem, it's time to step up and solve it. And the first thing a procrastinator wants to do is what? That's right, put it off!

Don't do that. You've taken the big step by acknowledging it's a problem. Now start dealing with it; don't put it off. Start solving the problem. To help, the ideas that follow will address some of the usual problems procrastinators have and provide you with strategies for dealing with them.

> ### *Assignment*
>
> Do something about your procrastination. Do it today. Do it now. Do it.

Epilogue

Recognizing it's a problem will not fix the problem. Look, it's different from a drug addiction or some other vice, but it IS stealing time from you and your family and causing unnecessary stress. Deal with it.

117

If It's on the To Do List, Do It

Elsewhere in this book I've written about To Do Lists. If you don't currently have one, make one. Nothing helps break the cycle of procrastination better that forcing yourself to live by a prioritized To Do List.

If you use it right, and discipline yourself to follow the rules of a To Do List, you have to work on projects and tasks in a priority order. So do that. Work down your list. When you come to an item that you are tempted to put off until another time—no matter the reason—don't. Follow the rules of the To Do List and do the task or project. That's the imposed discipline of the list.

Use that list to provide the artificial structure and discipline to do every task,

---

Assignment

Use a To Do List and make it your taskmaster. Follow it to the letter, one task at a time, until they are all done. No skipping allowed!

---

in order, on your list. If you do that, you'll find that you don't put things off. Tell yourself you are required to follow the list and have to do the task. Let the list be your taskmaster.

Epilogue

Psychologists tell us that sometimes people who procrastinate just need some external discipline to get them moving on a task. The To Do List can serve as that external motivation.

143

118

Commit to the Job—or Delegate It

When assigned a task or job, sometimes we just don't have the time to do it. For those who can, there are other options. If you are a supervisor, you do have some options to delegate the work to someone else who works for you. This can lighten your load and allow you more time, yet still gets the job accomplished.

However, any good supervisor has to realize that passing work to others could easily overload them, so caution is appropriate, and you will need a close awareness of the workloads of your staff. One way to manage it is to spread the elements of the job over a couple of people, perhaps including yourself. Then you just manage the job.

Assignment

When you receive work that will overload you, and you have the capability, delegate part or all of the job to others.

Remember, however, that delegating the work that was assigned to you does not mean you also delegate the responsibility for getting the job done. That was yours to begin with and remains yours even when you delegate the work to others.

Epilogue

Remember, though, that you are still responsible for that job getting done, so make sure it's still on your To Do List to check on. That's what being a supervisor is all about.

119

"It's Not My Job, Man!"

This has happened to all of us at one time or another: The boss comes in and assigns a task clearly the purview of someone else. And you're tempted to say, "But that's not my job!" Think before you do that.

Think about this situation for a minute. The boss may be assigning that task to you because he trusts you more than the person who is supposed to be doing the job—a plus for you,

> **Assignment**
>
> Critically assess these situations before jumping to one decision or another. Sometimes doing an unwanted task leads to other benefits.

and something you can use at your next job review. Or maybe the job really does belong to you or, if not, to no one and you just got selected.

In any event, first find a motivation to do the job before you try to get out of it. Trying to get out of it might be more damaging than just getting it done. What can motivate you? Perhaps it's avoiding the negative of not doing the job. Perhaps it's that your boss has asked YOU, not someone else. Perhaps it's because it's a job you can do better that anyone else. There can be lots of good reasons for taking on the task. Sometimes you may just have to find your own reason.

In the final analysis, is it going to be more time-consuming to get out of the job than to just do the job yourself? Decide.

> **Epilogue**
>
> A friend found herself in a similar situation—that is, assigned a task outside her area. But after reflection, she went forward and did a masterful job of it. That specific task turned out to be a trial for her. She was being tested—and she passed. It resulted in a promotion shortly thereafter.

120

Beat the Fear of the Unknown

Sometimes we are afraid of some jobs or tasks. What are the reasons?

Sometimes we are afraid of failing at a job that is new or risky. But failing is not necessarily bad. We can learn from failure. And who says it's going to be a failure anyway? If you change the fear to a positive attitude that you CAN do the job, the fear recedes.

Sometimes we fear what will happen when we succeed. If you think getting the job done well will then get you more such jobs, you fear success. Again, this is a positive. It means that you have carved out a niche that the organization sees of value and you are the "go-to" person.

> **Assignment**
>
> Don't allow your fears, whatever they might be, to keep you from success.

There are lots of other fears, but all of them can be defeated by a positive attitude. Find a way to turn each of these opportunities into a positive and then get the task done. Quite frankly, I have never been in an organization that has punished people for getting work done. So don't be afraid, just do it.

Epilogue

Remember that all the while you are agonizing over this job, you are using valuable time. Or losing valuable time. Or wasting valuable time.

121

Overcome the Insecurity of a Lack of Knowledge

You are uncertain about this job because you don't have any experience or not enough knowledge about the subject to feel confident.

This is an easy fear to overcome. Go out and get the knowledge you need. Sometimes that just means talking to someone who has done the work before. It might mean doing some reading up on the subject, or doing some research, or interviewing a few people to become smarter about the subject.

Although this all might take more time, it takes far

Assignment

Take the job, and get smart about it. Then get it done. It's that simple.

147

less time than the time you will spend worrying about the job and dithering about it. You'll just spin your wheels and go nowhere, continuing to waste time.

Epilogue

Never fear what you don't know, because in the 21st century, we have ready access to all kinds of information and knowledge. You just need to go out and get it.

122

If You Are Not Interested, Get Interested

Okay, sometimes the job just doesn't excite you. You're not really interest in it. It's boring. It's dull. It doesn't appear important enough.

Assignment

Don't rationalize this task away and let it just sit there because you aren't interested in it. It's similar to bad news: the older it gets, the smellier it gets.

If you think this way, you're in trouble. I have news for you: there are lots of jobs and tasks out there that you will not have much interest in doing. Tough! They need doing anyway.

If you get assigned one of those tasks that you are not interested in—get interested! Motivate yourself.

The tendency by procrastinators is to let these tasks just sit there. So they sit there and get old—and then older—and then someone asks about the task. Then you get nervous. Then someone asks again. And you worry about it all the time. Then your boss comes in to ask how that task is coming. And what do you say? You're working on it. Of course, you're not.

Don't let this happen to you. Find some motivation and get the work done. The motivation can even be negative motivation. You'll get in trouble if you don't get it done. You won't get promoted if you don't get it done.

Find a reason to get interested and quit procrastinating. Do the work.

Epilogue

Interest is not required to get work done—just the motivation to make it happen. All the while you are letting it sit there, you are worrying about it, thinking about it, and spending wasted time on it.

123

If You Don't Like the Task, Do It and It Will Go Away

Here's the easiest way to take care of this kind problem: if you really don't like a task, or don't want to do it, the fastest way to get rid of it is to get it done.

Yep, just do it and it will go away.

No more pain, no more worry, no more anxiety. All gone.

As they say at Nike: Just do it!

Assignment

The faster you get it done the sooner it will be out of the way and out of your life. Period.

Epilogue

Think of it as hitting your head against a wall: it feels so good when you stop, and the pain stops with it.

124

Schedule Travel Trips in Batches

Travel can be one of the most wasteful users of time we know. Unfortunately, we all have to do some of this. So it makes sense to make the best use of travel time as we can.

If you are traveling by car, try to build a schedule where you can put a couple (or more) of trips together into one travel segment. This minimizes your out-of-office time and makes for more efficient use of your time.

For example, if you need to visit with a client or customer, and stop by your accountant's office sometime that week, why not

Assignment

Look at batching your trips, both in and around town as well as long distance.

schedule them back-to-back? That allows you to make the best use of time away from your office—one trip instead of two. Most people save lots of time on local travel by batching their trips.

Of course, if you have to go long distance or are flying, do that same thing. Try to batch your visits into one trip instead of many small trips.

Epilogue

I've tested this idea on more than one occasion. Making just two stops during one trip instead of making two trips, I saved, on average, 45 minutes. Now that's time-saving!

125

Use Travel Time to Learn

We all have those longer trips where there is lots of "dead time" (time spent in airports, time on airplanes, time in hotels, and so forth). When this can't be avoided, use the time wisely. One of the best uses of this kind of time is to learn new skills.

I always conduct business travel with my notebook computer. And I always make a point of setting out to master a new set of skills during the trip. Sometimes I decide it's to learn more about a computer application, and I use help screens or tutorials. Sometimes I take a CD with some training modules on it to absorb.

Other times I take reading materials that have backed up over the past couple of weeks. Often, industry magazines back up on me so I take those on trips to get up to speed.

My notebook has "wi-fi" capability, so I will also do research on my destination, my client or customer, the city I'm traveling to, or any number of Internet things that add to my knowledge or abilities.

> **Assignment**
>
> Determine to use your "downtime" efficiently to learn new skills or gain knowledge. If not via a notebook computer, take a professional book or magazines with you. Be productive with this time.

Epilogue

The ideas that traveling is too hard and that you can't be productive on the road are nonsense. You can and should be productive, even if it's just to improve your capabilities. New capabilities or skills will save you time later.

126

Use Travel Time to Communicate

One of the easiest things to do while traveling is to talk to people. The modern cellular telephone allows us to keep in touch wherever we are, so why not use this time to make some contacts?

As you sit in that airport lounge waiting for that delayed flight, touch base with your office, call a couple of clients or customers, or call a colleague and discuss the state of the industry. Connect and make or maintain contacts with this downtime. Just remember to follow flight rules when on board an aircraft.

If you use a notebook computer with wi-fi capability, connect to the Internet and check and respond to e-mails so you are up to date when you return.

If you are driving, you can still do the same thing. Call the office, call your appointment to confirm—or to tell him you are stuck behind an accident and might be a little late—call appointments for the next day to confirm. There are lots of people you could use this time to touch base with while driving.

One note of caution while driving: always use a hands-free device. Doing so is much safer than trying to hold that phone to your ear, and allows you to drive with both hands. There are all types available today, and many are very inexpensive. I use one routinely that I got as a part of my last cellular contract. It works great, I communicate better using it, and I probably drive better, too.

> ### Assignment
>
> While traveling, plan some communication on the way to and from. Again, make use of this time and it will save you time later.

Epilogue

All this talking will save you time later when you have to make the same calls from the office. You could be doing other things and get home on time that day.

127

Use Travel Time to Unwind

Sometimes you are traveling after a hard day's or week's work and face a stressful trip and more work at the other end. When this happens to me, I often resolve to relax and unwind while traveling. I know, it's not getting anything done, but it is helping me recover from stress and allowing me to be better prepared, rested, and refreshed for the coming event.

Assignment

When you are stressed, and time allows it, relax during travel time. Unwind and de-stress. Be better prepared for your arrival event.

If you are traveling by car, take a book tape or CD and listen to it while you drive. Listen to your favorite music or talk show. If you are traveling by air, take a good novel and immerse yourself in it for a few hours. Take a portable CD player or an iPod or MP3 player and listen to music.

Relax, unwind, and refresh yourself so you will be better prepared both physically and mentally for the next meeting or event you are traveling to.

Epilogue

Though this does not save you time immediately, it will save you time later as you arrive refreshed and better able to handle what comes your way at the other end.

128

Use Travel Time to Prepare

One great use of travel time, which is most applicable to air travel, is preparation for the upcoming event or meeting you are traveling to. Sitting in airports and on airplanes is very conducive to reading and making notes.

I do this all the time when traveling. I know that I will have time while I travel, so I put all my advanced reading into a folder to review while I'm traveling. That way I'm using my office time efficiently, but I am also using my travel time to my best advantage.

> ### Assignment
>
> When using air travel, take all your preparation materials with you. Then read them in the airport and on the plane.

This also has the advantage of allowing that information to be fresh for me when I arrive and need to use it.

Epilogue

This saves you time at the office and efficiently uses your travel time to your best advantage.

129

Use Airplane Time to Catch Up

If you fall behind on tasks as I often do, traveling usually provides some uninterrupted time to get caught up on things. This is especially true for air travel where there is a lot of time just sitting around.

When I get into these situations, I pack a couple of folders with materials I want to read or work on, toss my notebook computer over my shoulder, and hit the road. While waiting in the airport, or while sitting on the plane, I can break open the files and read, write, take notes—whatever. If I need to do work on the computer, I simply fire up the notebook and go to work.

This is a great use of time that otherwise would be unproductive.

> **Assignment**
>
> Determine to use travel time to catch up, or even get ahead, on work.

Epilogue

This technique will save you time by allowing you fairly uninterrupted time to do work—either catching up or getting ahead.

130

Use Travel Time to Read

Remember all that reading you had to figure out when to do? Those trade magazines, internal reports, research reports, and so forth? Well, traveling is a great time to do all that reading. Not while you are driving the car, no, but when you are in an airport, on the plane, in the hotel, or in a taxi on the way somewhere.

All of these opportunities are times to get caught up on your professional reading.

Quite frankly, the best times I have for this kind of reading is when I'm on the road.

Assignment

Take your "catch-up reading" with you when you travel and use that time to get caught up. Don't just sit there looking out the window.

Epilogue

You know you need to read all that stuff and will be behind if you don't, so take it with you and use your travel time. Again, it saves you time later.

131

Set Personal and Family Goals

Your personal life should be a part of your time planning and management as well as your professional life. After all, it is a major part of your day, week, and month.

As you decide what goals you want to set for your professional life, don't forget your personal life as well. Your long-range goals should include some personal goals as well—goals such as when you want to retire; how many kids you want and to what extent you want to support them in college; and any goals relating to yourself, such as home purchase, education, spouse education, and so forth.

Assignment

When outlining your long-range goals and short-term objectives, always include personal and family goals and objectives so you can plan for them.

Your objectives for each year should also include personal objectives, such as spending time at home with family, or vacation time, or participating in your children's activities at home and at school. Include these so you can plan time to actually accomplish them.

Epilogue

If you don't include this stuff, you'll never get to do it. They have to be in your plan. Your financial advisor is going to ask the same kinds of questions of you when it's time to talk to one, so start now.

132

Make Certain You Leave Time for Personal Goals

Okay, good start. You have outlined long-range goals and short-term objectives that involve you and your family. Now make certain you include time every day and every week and every month to actually accomplish those things.

> ### *Assignment*
>
> Every day ask yourself the question: "Am I including anything today that helps me accomplish my personal or family goals and objectives?"

The reason I recommend these be written down is so they can be reviewed routinely and then acted upon. So, when you are looking over that work schedule for tomorrow and realize that you have a child's piano recital that evening, and you note that one of your goals was to be involved in your children's lives—well, you know what you need to do. Get that recital on your calendar for tomorrow!

If you don't plan for these things to happen, they won't happen. So include them in all your daily planning.

Epilogue

Of course, you can't always accommodate something every day, but the process is to ask the question every day so that you do, over time, get these things done.

133

Schedule Downtime During the Day

All of you A personality types out there, listen up! You will burn yourself out if you don't relax a little. Studies have shown that the more you work without breaks, the less effective and efficient you are. So learn from the research and plan for some downtime during every day.

How? The first tactic is to leave the office and have lunch every day away from your desk. Okay, you diehards, you can still take your lunch in a brown bag, but go outside (in good weather) and relax by the lake or outside of the office. Take a half hour and think about something other than work.

Assignment

Schedule downtime every day. It doesn't have to be a lot of time—indeed it should probably not be a lot of time. But a little break from the work goes a long way to refreshing your mind.

Another way is to schedule some of that reading time every day. We've addressed how to handle all that reading you have to do, but one way is to simply allocate a half hour every day, perhaps in the afternoon, to get that reading taken care of. It's often relaxing and serves to de-stress you. You come back to the work a little refreshed and ready for more.

Take a couple of breaks during the day.

Go have a brief chat with a colleague for five minutes.

Even a little time away from the "grindstone" will help you come back refreshed and ready for more. And you'll be more effective and more efficient because of it.

Epilogue

The research is quite clear: We are refreshed even with small breaks in the work schedule, and we are also more efficient when we return to the tasks at hand.

134

Take Brief Breaks

Another thing to do to refresh yourself is to take brief breaks throughout the day. No, not those 20-minute smoke breaks others take. Another thing to do is take a five-minute break every couple of hours.

Sometimes these just happen naturally, such as when you drive 10 minutes to get to an appointment or walk to the next building on campus to meet someone.

But more often, you have to make these opportunities, or plan them.

What kind of breaks? How about a quick walk to the soda machine for your favorite soda? Or a trip to the coffee pot for another cup of joe in the morning (my favorite)? Or go visit

> ### *Assignment*
>
> Make yourself take brief breaks throughout the day. Not long, perhaps five minutes or so. Almost anything not specifically related to your work will do.

a friend in another office for five minutes to talk about the kids. Or just sit at your desk and surf the net for your next vacation spot for five minutes. Or—well, you get the drift.

Epilogue

These breaks serve to refresh you and serve as great mental transition devices to move to the next project.

135

Don't Overwork Yourself

I have a friend who I expect to lose early in her life. Yep, she's a classic workaholic. She spends 12–14 hours every day at work, then invests another four hours at home or with family activities. That's 16–18 hours she's is engaged fully every day.

And none of this activity is for herself. She's overworking herself. To her credit, she knows this about herself and is working to overcome this problem. But she is likely to burn herself out early in life.

Don't let this happen to you. In addition to burnout, studies of employees who work those kinds of hours routinely indicate that the last few hours are very unproductive. They also show that's when mistakes are made.

It's because people are tired and not on their "A Game."

Don't let this happen to you. Working an eight- to 10-hour day efficiently, using the techniques from this book, should be plenty to get the job done.

Assignment

Target your workday to eight to 10 hours. Only work longer by exception, not as a rule. Stay on your A Game.

> **Epilogue**
>
> *It's really hard to watch these people burn themselves out. And also to know they will probably have to rework all the tasks they handled during the last few hours of working because they were not at their best.*

136

Schedule Medical and Dental Visits Well in Advance

Here's a good time-saving tip. We all have to see doctors and dentists on some regular basis. As we get older, perhaps it's more often. These activities can be scheduled and should never be left until the last minute.

The problem with all too many people is that they wait until the last minute to make that appointment. Then they are trying to

Assignment

Plan for doctor and dentist appointments at least two weeks in advance. Get them scheduled and on your calendar. Then they are fully planned events you can schedule around effectively without fragmenting your day.

sandwich in an appointment to an already-busy day and, by the time they finally call, only a few appointment times are available.

This increases stress and complicates—and fragments—the workday.

So plan for these events well in advance and schedule when it is most advantageous to you, not fit in between other activities.

Epilogue

Sorry, but yes: you have to see the dentist at least a couple times a year. So plan ahead so it doesn't screw up your schedule and make the day even more difficult.

137

Schedule Medical and Dental Visits for Early Morning

A great trick with these appointments is to set them in advance and for first thing in the morning. For example, my family doctor starts appointments at 7 a.m. I always schedule myself for appointments with him for that time by scheduling in advance.

That way, I'm first and not delayed, as many appointments later in the day can be, and I'm done and out of there and to work nearly on time. Mission accomplished, and no impact on my work.

I schedule my dentist the same way, although she doesn't start until 8 a.m. Still, I'm minimizing my time away from the office, and I make certain that these appointments don't fragment my day by being in the middle of the morning or afternoon.

Assignment

Schedule your medical and dental appointments at the beginning of the day or the end of the day.

Epilogue

The key here is to keep from fragmenting your day with these appointments. You don't want to have to stop work, go to the appointment, and then start up work again.

138

Grocery Trips: Buy Bulk

In this quick shop culture, this idea may be a lead balloon. Nonetheless, I'll try to make this point clear. Every time you break into your day for a simple, unplanned task, you fragment your day and cause inefficiency.

So, every time you have to run to the store for a carton of milk, or an ingredient for a baking project, you are fragmenting your day's work. Every time you have to run to the supply closet for more paper for the printer, or try to find a new printer cartridge, you are fragmenting your day.

When you buy groceries, buy bulk. Get lots of stuff. Stock the pantry. Don't end up having to make multiple trips to the store every week just for one or two items. This just fragments all of your efforts.

The same is true at work. Have your supplies on hand, not at the store or in the supply room. When you start a project, have everything you need at hand so you don't have to stop and go get something or, worse, go buy something.

Assignment

Buy bulk, and prepare for your projects. Don't get into a situation where you are constantly running out the get something.

Epilogue

Fragmenting your work and life effort simply delays things and uses extra time. Save time by having it all there when you need it.

139

Organize the Closet

Sometimes the time we spend getting ready to do things at home costs us time it should not. One area for you to look is your closet. Yep, the place where we hang and store clothes. If you are taking time finding the right clothing every morning, then you are likely wasting time. Yes, it might only be five minutes, but five minutes times five days times four weeks adds up to 100 minutes a month. That's more than an hour and a half each month you've wasted searching for your clothes.

Seemed silly at first, didn't it? Not so silly now! An hour and a half is a substantial amount of time.

So, get that closet organized. Put your work clothes in one area. Your play stuff, gardening stuff, and you sports stuff go somewhere special. Get it organized. Organize those shoes. Organize those drawers so your work stuff is easily at hand.

> ### Assignment
>
> Organize your closet. Be prepared to find what you need quickly and efficiently.

Epilogue

It seems silly, but it will save you time every day, every week, every month.

140

Don't Make Special Trips— Combine Them

Too many times I watch people make special trips for one or two items, or, I see them schedule appointments out of the office once a day. As with all such things, it just fragments the day more and makes you more inefficient.

Combine all your trips out of the office—and out of the home—into one large trip or a couple of combined trips.

For example, I don't run errands every day. All my errands are done on Saturday morning. I group all the trips together into one series of stops. By noon on Saturday I'm done. Every errand is run, everything is put away (yes, even groceries), and I'm on to other things.

Now, my neighbors—well, that's different. Their car leaves the garage every Saturday about 10 times. And they come back with one or two things. They even do this during the week. They will come home from work. Run an errand. Eat dinner. Run an errand.

What fragmentation!

Combine these trips into one large, efficient trip where you get it all done. Then you can move on to other, perhaps more enjoyable, things. Maybe a softball game followed by a BBQ. Now you're talking!

Assignment

Group your errands into one large trip. Not only will you save time, but you'll be much more efficient and get everything done faster.

Epilogue

This takes planning. So plan these things and save some time.

141

Organize and Systemize Your Morning Procedure

For some people, every morning is an adventure. They are unorganized and chaotic. Everyone is rushing around with no system and getting in each other's way. All this chaos and disorder costs time. It is also quite stressful and a terrible way to start your day.

Consider establishing a system, a routine, to your morning preparations.

Scheduling people seems over-controlling, but in large families it is necessary. My father grew up in a family of six kids, all two years apart in age. Without a system, they would never have gotten out the door in the morning. But it is even important for small households. There are only two people in my house, but we have a simple system of getting out the door in the morning without getting in each other's way. No chaos; it's organized.

Assignment

Set up a system for your mornings so you can efficiently get out the door.

The system should be quite simple. Sometimes simply having people rise a few minutes apart and putting everyone into a sequence that best uses the homes facilities is the easiest way to do it. You can base that on who has to get out the door first in the morning.

169

> **Epilogue**
> *Everyone's system will be different, but having one is important. Not only does it efficiently get you started, but it does so without a lot of stress. Start your day refreshed, not stressed!*

142

Train the Family

Yep, it takes training. Once your system is in place, it doesn't just happen—especially if there are children in the family. Just telling them what to do isn't enough for youngsters. You need to train them and sometimes supervise them.

Assignment

Walk everyone through the process. Make sure everyone knows his or her role and why you are doing it this way.

Get them trained and used to a routine and it will all work smoothly. Yes, there will be some occasional wrinkles and changes. But overall, you need a system that works, and people who work the system.

> **Epilogue**
> *Get family members to understand that it is part of their responsibility to help the family get organized and going every morning.*

143

Reward Yourself

Sometimes the best rewards are not those that come from others, but those that we give to ourselves. When things go as planned, when you get tasks and projects done on time, reward yourself.

Here's a story: When I was a smoker (reformed and fairly intolerant now!) I used to complete a task or project and reward myself with a cigarette. The cigarette was my way of signaling accomplishment and obtaining reward. I could not have the cigarette until the task was complete. Later, I changed that to small candies. Later still, I changed that to a cup of coffee. And finally, I rewarded myself with a short break.

> ### Assignment
>
> Establish a simple reward system for yourself to encourage efficiency and good time use.

Those all worked for me. They kept me on task and were quite simple (yeah, the cigarettes were deadly, but…) to provide.

Find a similar system for yourself. It keeps you efficient, keeps you on task, and uses time wisely. And the reward should be something brief and easy to do.

Epilogue

We all work for rewards of some kind: the reward of a raise, or promotion, or seeing success. This little system just uses our natural human tendencies. And it works.

144

Don't Be a Perfectionist

Mrs. Smith, your 5th-grade teacher, is going to cringe when I say this, but: not everything has to be perfect.

What? Tell me it ain't so!

Sorry, there are just some things that don't have to be better than just okay. Sometimes the minimum is just fine. Don't try to get an A on every paper, so to speak.

Of course, only you can know what those things truly are, but, for example, personal notes from a meeting don't have to be typed up if only for yourself. Routine reports are often just that: routine. So just get them done. Don't spend more time on them than necessary.

Save quality time and quality work for the high-priority tasks and projects where it can make a difference.

> ### Assignment
>
> Do routine things routinely. Don't spend more time than is necessary on things that simply don't require it.

Epilogue

Save time for the things that matter. On those things, don't skimp. Give them your best work. On the routine stuff, just give 'em what is necessary.

145

Home Communication: Are You Over-Connected?

We all have a lot of communication going on at home—sometimes too much. Let's see what's available. First, of course, is the telephone; and of course everyone has a cell phone. Then there is the TV—or TVs. How about computers? And the Internet connections? Fast? Yep.

Assignment

Control the use of communication and entertainment activities at home. Use some of that time to do some family activities, take care of some household chores, or work on your "honey do" list.

So how does all this communication impact your time? It owns it! Think about your home and all the communication devices you have that can attract your time the way flypaper attracts flies. Sometimes all this communication leads to overload. We spend so much time communicating that we don't get everything done.

Camped out watching baseball or football all weekend? What else did you get done?

Butt sore from surfing the Internet all weekend? What else did you get done?

Played video games and kicked butt all weekend? What else did you get done?

It's fine to have all this stuff. And great relaxation. But don't end up letting this communicating world control your life every night or all weekend. Practice some self-control and get some of that other stuff done, too.

Epilogue

Time is the thing that we run out of. Once it's gone, it cannot be replaced. Use it wisely.

146

TV Time Sucks Away From People Time

Speaking of television…

That thing will suck the life out of you! Get control now. Just coming home and plopping down in front of the tube to vegetate is not living. It's going brain dead. You get nothing accomplished.

But wait, you say. We watch TV as a family. No, you don't! You just happen to sit in the same room together, but the experiences are individual. There's little interaction, little discussion, and little, if any, brain matter being used, either.

Assignment

Limit your time in front of the tube. Watch what is appropriate and quality, and spend the rest of the time on family goals and objectives.

Limit your time in front of the TV. Limit kids' time, too. Do things as a family. Go somewhere. Work on a family project. In the evening, get some work done on family goals and objectives; don't leave them all for the weekend.

Use your time at home for something besides disappearing into the television.

Epilogue

Television is an incredible time-waster. Most of what we watch is garbage. We get little from it. Watch the good stuff, ignore the rest, and find something productive to do.

147

Control Children's Access to TV

Children, too, waste a lot of time in front of that tube. If research is correct, the average kid watches nearly five hours of television a day. A day!

There simply is not enough quality programming on any given day to justify five hours.

Assignment

Offer some alternatives to television and encourage children to do things that are more engaging or productive.

Encourage your children to do things other than watch television. (The Internet is not an alternative!) Encourage them to play games, do homework, interact with other kids, get involved in community projects, or even read a book.

Don't let their brains get wasted by television and let their time get wasted by this voracious monster.

Epilogue

Research is beginning to demonstrate that there is a correlation between children's time watching television and lower test scores. And it's a terrible waste of their precious time in their formative years.

148

Control Children's Access to the Internet

By now you know that dangers lurk on the Internet. Camping out on the Net usually is entertainment, not learning. Perhaps just as importantly, there are lots of problems and

Assignment

Keep control of the Internet, and keep your kids safe and spending their time wisely.

dangers out there for children with unrestricted access to the Internet.

You should control this access to supervise not only the content they view, but also the time they spend on the Net.

Some close friends with three boys put their computer with Internet access in the family room. The rule was that the boys could get on the Internet only after their homework was done, only for an hour, and a parent had to be in the room.

Epilogue

Is this one going to save you time? Yes. If you have kids who get addicted to the Internet and neglect their schoolwork, you'll have to intervene. It's better to keep that from happening.

149

Don't Check Your Portfolio Every Day

I have a friend, Tom, who does his own investing. He has an account with one of the online brokers and manages his own portfolio. I think he's pretty good at it.

He has only one problem: he's doing it all the time. At work, he's constantly checking stock prices. Over lunch, he's doing research on his stocks or potential stock to buy. At home he spends at least an hour every night at this task. I'd bet he spends at least two and a half hours a day at this.

It's probably not an addiction and not a major problem if he's doing well (and I think he is). The problem is in the fragmenting of his time this does every day.

I stick my head in the door of his office and he's checking stock prices. He then goes back to work and has to reorient himself on the task or project he's working on. It fragments his concentration and costs him time.

> ### Assignment
>
> If you do your own investing online, control your urge to check on the investments every 10 minutes and stay concentrated on your tasks.

To be successful at this, he doesn't have to check every few minutes. A couple times each day will likely do just fine.

Epilogue

Tom kills a lot of time doing this. He would probably save himself an hour a day if he just limited his reviews to once each morning and once each afternoon.

150

Schedule Vacations—and Take Them!

Vacations are important. That's why companies give you that time. It's time to relax, regenerate, rejuvenate, and reenergize yourself.

But too many people don't take their vacation time and end up tired, and overwhelmed by work, and they never get refreshed.

My friend and colleague Sally is one of those people. She mentioned the other day that she has so much vacation time built up that she is losing it every year. Of course, I took her to task about that.

Losing vacation time can be thought of as giving away money! You get this time as part of your compensation. It's there for a reason. Your company wants you to take that time so you can be refreshed and a better employee and member of the team.

The more tired you get, the more inefficient you get. Inefficiency costs you time. Vacations let you rest up both physically and mentally.

Assignment

Take those vacations. You'll be more efficient when you return. Your family will appreciate it, too.

Epilogue

People who don't take vacations have been studied. They tend to be more inefficient than most, be more tired than most, and burn out earlier on various jobs than most. Don't let this happen to you.

151

Try to Live Close to Work

Okay, not everyone can just up and move. If you are in a situation where you can, then consider moving closer to work.

Why? Some people in California are now commuting more than an hour one way to get to their work. In Los Angeles this may not be helped given the cost of housing people, but that's not true in all cities, and it may not be in yours.

Assignment

If you are in a position to do so, consider moving closer to your workplace.

Many cities are seeing a resurgence of urban living. Apartments and condos are being built especially for people who do have the capacity to move to be closer to work. For people who's children are grown and out of the house, this is a perfect solution.

If you save just 10 minutes on your morning commute by moving closer to work, you will save 20 minutes a day, 100 minutes a week, and 400 minutes a month. That's more than six and a half hours a month you would save!

Epilogue

Who wouldn't like to have more than six extra hours a month available for other things?

Index

About the Author

Bob Dittmer has more than 25 years of experience in public relations, marketing, and higher education.

He currently serves as a faculty member in the School of Journalism at Indiana University, Purdue University, Indianapolis, after more than 15 years as an adjunct faculty member with colleges and universities around the country, in both graduate and undergraduate programs. He teaches public relations courses, is responsible for managing the public relations sequence, and serves as the marketing and retention officer for the school.

He has served as the director of media relations for both an American government organization with responsibilities for all of Europe, as well as for a major NATO organization with responsibilities for public information management worldwide. Bob has more than 15 years experience in public relations and advertising agencies, working on a wide variety of clients in both business-to-business and business-to-consumer arenas. He is also an author and literary agent.

With a B.A. from John Carroll University and an M.A. in Communication from Marshall University, and accreditation from the Public Relations Society of America (PRSA), he is also dedicated to his profession. He was the 1998 President of the Hoosier (Indiana) Chapter, PRSA. He also served as 1999 Chair of PRSA's National Association Section and as Chair of PRSA's East Central District in 2001 (five states) and remains on the Board of Directors of the Hoosier Chapter. Bob was elected to membership in the Indianapolis Public Relations Society in 1998.

Bob has spent years experiencing and examining almost every kind of time-waster you can imagine. Over the years he has collected the ideas he and others have developed to solve these time challenges. This has led to the book *151 Quick Ideas to Manage Your Time*. He is currently at work editing another of the 151 Quick Ideas books as well as co-writing another book on writing.

Bob and his wife, Susan, live in Indianapolis.